Cell Leader
Intern
Guidebook

The Critical Path
for Successful Leadership

CELL LEADER INTERN GUIDEBOOK
previously titled
MANUAL FOR TRAINING CELL LEADERS

©1995 by TOUCH Publications, Inc.

ACKNOWLEDGEMENTS:

This training manual is developed from a summary and adaptation of the following books by the pastoral team of Hatfield Christian Church, Pretoria, South Africa:

1. *The Shepherd's Training Manual,* by Ralph W. Neighbour, Jr.
2. *Cell Leader's Guidebook,* compiled by Ong Swee Geok; edited by Ralph W. Neighbour, Jr. (Available from Touch Resource, #06-00/07-00, 66-68 East Coast Road, Singapore 1542)
3. *The Home Group* by Hatfield Christian Church, Pretoria, South Africa.

It contains concepts and diagrams contributed by Bill Beckham, Eugene Seow, and Dion Robert. Additional contributions have been provided by Ralph W. Neighbour, Jr., Jim Egli and other staff of TOUCH Outreach Ministries. No royalty will be paid to anyone from the sale of this book. It is a gift of love to the cell church movement.

Distributors include:

TOUCH Publications, Inc., P.O. Box 19888, Houston, Texas, 77224-9888 USA
Telephone 713-497-7901
Fax 713-497-0904
Internet <touchusa@riter.computize.com>

TOUCH International South Africa, P.O. Box 1223, Newcastle 2940, South Africa
Telephone (03431) 28111
Fax (03431) 24211

Printed in the United States of America

CONTENTS

PREFACE

For a number of years cell groups have played an important role in the life of our church. They have formed part of the strategy given to us by the Lord to effectively care for our members. However, cell groups should have a twofold thrust: ministry and nurture within the church, as well as ministry and outreach to the communities in which we live.

Cells form the basic building blocks of church life. They are the very heartbeat of the church. I believe that a cell group church with this twofold objective will experience dynamic growth.

One of the major shortcomings in the church at large has been the inadequate equipping of church members for ministry. As a result, we have robbed our people of the blessing of ministering to the needs of others, and leaders have also been released without proper training, making their task that much more difficult.

Dr. Ralph Neighbour, Jr. has written extensive material on how to train leaders and equip people for ministry. This book is a summary of certain of his material. It will enable pastors to more effectively train their cell leaders for the work of the ministry. A sincere word of thanks is extended to Dr. Neighbour for allowing us to use and adapt his books to suit our particular situation.

Training and structures have always had limited success. The material in this book will only be effective if implemented under the guidance and in the power of the Holy Spirit. Only a total openness to the flow of the Spirit will ensure ministry in the cells that will change lives.

I have found that church members have a deep desire to be used by God. They know that they have the "words of life" and long to reach out and touch hurting people, but often don't know how to do it. This manual can help you. Prayerfully consider its contents and count the cost of change. Do not be tempted to rush your church into major change. Rather, spend months or even years in adequate preparation and training and then take your entire congregation with you into this new approach.

Churches across the world are returning to the biblical model written about in the book of Acts. The fresh outpouring of the Holy Spirit across the earth, and the worldwide explosion of cell group churches are both supernatural phenomena. Revival is at our door! The church is being renewed!

Where the Spirit of the Lord is, there is liberty. We welcome Him to renew His Body, to change us and the form our churches take. As we encounter the new wine of the Spirit we are expecting an unprecedented harvest!

Pastor Ed Roebert,
Senior Pastor
Hatfield Christian Church
Pretoria, South Africa

INTRODUCTION

It was He who gave some to be apostles, some to be prophets, some to be evangelists, and some to be pastors and teachers, to prepare God's people for works of service, so that the body of Christ may be built up until we all reach unity in the faith and in the knowledge of the Son of God and become mature, attaining to the whole measure of the fullness of Christ. (Ephesians 4:11-13)

Welcome to your new ministry! You are about to become the primary care giver to a group of up to 15 persons. They will model your lifestyle, learning how to serve the Lord by observing you. This might be frightening except for one fact: *Christ dwells in you!* His life brings to you His righteousness. As you seek to serve others, always be in contact with the Holy Spirit who empowers you.

You are not embarking on this ministry as a novice. During the past months as a cell member you have been shaping your value system and learning to win "Type A" and "Type B" unbelievers to Christ. You have served as a Sponsor to at least one other person. You have seen at least one other person accept Christ as Lord and enter your Cell Group. You have experienced the power of God. You may even have spiritual "battle scars" from learning how to combat Satan's power, both in strongholds in your life and in the lives of others.

This Guidebook is designed to help you prepare for ministry as a Cell Leader. You are to read each of the eight chapters *in advance* of attending the training sessions.

Your Cell Leader, Zone Supervisor, Zone Pastor, and trainer will be at your side, modeling what you are being trained to do. Following the eight weeks of orientation, special Cell Leader Advanced Modules will be offered as electives. Choose those of interest to you.

These next two months will be very, very special for you. It may require you to cut back on other priorities to focus on your training. Throw yourself into this equipping with all your heart! As in all training, your *concentration* is as important as the *new information* you will receive.

HOW TO USE THIS BOOK

This book is intended to prepare you for your training sessions. Before each session, you are required to read the next chapter in this book to prepare you for the training you will receive. There are also reading assignments to be completed in the *Shepherd's Guidebook* and *Ordering Your Private World*. These are crucial to the development of your character and your ministry. Take these reading assignments seriously!

The training sessions will assume you have done this preparation, and will then seek to give you experience in leading a cell. The goal is to provide experience-based training as opposed to knowledge-based training. Your sessions will be conducted by a trainer in the setting of a simulated cell group. If the class is larger than 15, the group can be addressed as a whole by the trainer and then be divided into smaller groups to continue the activities.

You will be given specific responsibilities to do during the meetings. This "hands-on" training will strengthen your ministry.

YOU WILL DEVELOP A PARTNER RELATIONSHIP

Your trainer will assign you to another Cell Leader Intern at the beginning of the course. The two of you will function as partners to each other. You are required to develop this relationship. The materials that you will need to cover will be given to you during this course.

YOU WILL REMAIN DEEPLY INVOLVED WITH UNBELIEVERS

You are required to identify two unbelievers in your *"oikos"* and start praying for opportunities to share John 3:16 with them. Deepen your relationship with them and make an effort to have social contact with them. One of the most important parts of your internship is to learn how to stay involved with unbelievers. The most dangerous cell leader is one who has so concentrated on the people *inside* the cell that the unreached world is forgotten. Remember that the only way a cell group grows is through bringing people to Jesus and then into the fellowship of the Basic Christian Community.

SCHEDULE FOR THE CELL LEADER INTERN WEEKEND

FIRST DAY, 7-10 P.M.

7:00	Informal Fellowship
7:30	Praise and Worship
7:45	Cell Leader Profile presented; review of books:

        Cell Leader Intern Guidebook
        The Shepherd's Guidebook (see page 12)
        Ordering Your Private World

8:10   Panel: a week in the life of a Cell Group Leader
        Panel Participants: three veteran cell leaders, one Zone Supervisor

8:30   Small Group discussion with your Zone Pastor

8:45   The DISC Relationship Survey
        Videotape: *How to use the DISC Test*
        Instructions for taking and grading the test. You will take it on your own prior to returning to the Saturday session.

9:25   Small Group discussion with your Zone Pastor

9:40   Break into triads for closing prayer time

SECOND DAY, 12-7:45 P.M.

12:00   Agape Meal: led by Zone Pastor(s)

1:00   DISCUSSION: Sources of Assistance for your ministry:
        1. Your Zone Supervisor
        2. Your Zone Pastor

1:30   Small Group discussion with your Zone Pastor

1:50   Wives and husbands meet separately: "My calling"

2:20   WHAT TO DO WHEN YOU HAVE:
        1. A death call
        2. A member living in sin
        3. A complaining cell member
        4. A marital crisis
        5. An unexpected visitor (unsaved?)

3:30   BREAK

4:00	How to find potential Cell Leader Interns as *you* intern
4:15	Small group discussion with your Zone Pastor
4:30	How to baptize (swim suits required)
5:45	Dinner hour
6:30	Your first assignments for the eight weeks of training *(Presented by your Zone Pastor)*
6:45	Vision Casting, testimonies, edification time
7:45	Dismiss

SUNDAY WORSHIP SERVICE

You will be presented in the Celebration worship service. You may be asked to prepare a 1-2 minute testimony. You will be set aside in prayer for your internship.

CELL LEADER PROFILE

Biblical Background:

The book of Acts reveals that house groups formed the first church life. The very first day after Pentecost, there were 3,120 believers moving from house to house. Averaging 10 to a house, there were approximately 312 home groups. We know that a key part of every home group meeting was the observation of the *"agape* feast," for we are told they "broke bread" from house to house. This was the Lord's supper.

Jesus had given the commandment to perform this ritual until He returned. Thus, we know the first house groups regularly observed this sacred meal. It may have been done every time they met in a home to share in worship and edification. We know there were also unbelievers and "ungifted ones" present in these small groups; undoubtedly they were impacted by observing the sharing of the bread and the cup among the believers. This memorial meal clearly taught the importance of the crucifixion of Christ for the redemption of all men. Scripture never tells us what a *diakone* did, because the very name tells us what this person did! The ministry was to serve the Lord's Supper to the members in the home group.

9

The special person who served this meal, who broke the bread and served the cup, was a substitute for the Christ who served these elements at the Last Supper. It is believed that the term "deacon," *diakone*—literally, *"table waiter,"* refers to a Spirit-filled person in the early church who filled this role in each cell group. *For every home group, there would be one person who would serve the Lord's Supper.*

Therefore, the position we call "Cell Leader" is an antiseptic, unscriptural term that is "safe" to use in our mixed-up period of church history. Today, deacons are often given jobs which cannot be confirmed by any portion of scripture. In reality, we should go ahead and call every cell leader by the biblical term *deacon,* but tradition is hard to break. The verses below apply to men or women and provide us with a description of the *character* of a deacon. Consider these words to be proper for evaluating a cell leader as well:

1 Timothy 3:8-11: Deacons, likewise, are to be men worthy of respect, sincere, not indulging in much wine, and not pursuing dishonest gain. They must keep hold of the deep truths of the faith with a clear conscience. They must first be tested; and then if there is nothing against them, let them serve as deacons. In the same way, their wives are to be women worthy of respect, not malicious talkers but temperate and trustworthy in everything. A deacon must be the husband of but one wife and must manage his children and his household well. Those who have served well gain an excellent standing and great assurance in their faith in Christ Jesus.

1. PROFILE OF A CELL GROUP LEADER

  1. CHARACTER
    A. 1 Timothy 3:8-14 is our guide. Consider this to be one of the most challenging periods of your life! A good motto to remember might be, "the best ability is *dependability.*"
    B. You will be lovingly "tested" by your Cell Leader, Zone Supervisor, or Zone Pastor during these weeks.

C. Any of these means of "testing" may be used during the weeks of your orientation:
   a. You may be asked to conduct early morning Bible studies with potential interns.
   b. You may be asked to do a budget sheet of your personal finances.
   c. Submissiveness might be tested by giving tasks you don't like and watching how you react.
   d. Knowing you only cognitively may be very dangerous to those you are shepherding!
      1. You will be given "experiences" to do to evaluate how you perform. These will be prayerfully presented to challenge you.
      2. You may be assigned interviews with incoming cell members or with Type "B" unbelievers.
      3. Your reading assignments in *The Shepherd's Guidebook* and *Ordering Your Private World* will be evaluated.
   e. Faithfulness in little things will be observed.
   f. Your values will be evaluated.
   g. Your prayer life will be considered.
   h. Frank discussions of sexual temptations and how you have handled them in the past may be expected.
   i. Is your husband/wife fully committed to the Lordship of Christ?
D. Your commitment to the ministry will be considered.
   a. How disciplined are you?
   b. How available is your time?
   c. Are you serving to get personal attention or to serve Christ?

2. SKILLS
   A. In terms of the "D-I-S-C" profile:
      a. You will be helped to serve your Lord within the parameters of the way you are created by God.
      b. You will be encouraged to take the DISC test in another six months to discover how ministry has impacted you.

B. Spiritual skills needed:
 a. Flowing in the gifts.
 b. Sensitive to God.
 c. Prophetic.
 d. Worship Leader.
 e. Harvester of the Lost.
C. Relational Skills:
 a. Gifted in group dynamics.
 b. Capable of conflict resolution.
D. Organizational Skills:
 a. Motivator (especially for "Share The Vision" times).
 b. Know how to delegate to cell members.
 c. Faithfully contact members.
 d. Careful to develop a potential Intern properly.
E. Counseling Skills
 a. Know when to make referrals.
 b. Able to listen effectively.
 c. Do not "lecture" or "scold" when someone shares deeply.
F. Knowledge
 a. Have a clearly defined ecclesiology of Cell Group Church Life.
 b. Understand the ordinances of baptism and the Lord's Supper.
 c. Be able to express how one receives salvation by faith using the John 3:16 diagram.
 d. Understand how to share sanctification truths.
 e. Know and experience "signs and wonders," or "power encounters."

2. A REVIEW OF THE SHEPHERD'S GUIDEBOOK

(Note: this is used the first night of the Cell Leader Intern Weekend. Each person should have a copy of the Shepherd's Guidebook.)

INTRODUCTION:
As an Intern, this book is your handbook. It has been prepared exclusively for your use. During the six months or so that you will be interning, you will use it to shape your *life* and your *ministry*. Let's take a look at how it performs these two tasks:

1. SHAPING YOUR LIFE
   A. Your personal lifestyle is covered in Part One.
   B. In this book, you are called a "Shepherd." Don't be fooled by thinking this term is "out of style" or "not appropriate for an urban world!" The Bible is a timeless book, and the constant use of "shepherd" to refer to your ministry has a very deep truth behind it.
      - A Shepherd, first of all, is a *responsible* person. This responsibility increases with your maturity as a servant of God. For example, let's look at John 21:
        v. 15: *"Tend my lambs"* refers to the work of a child, not an adult.
        v. 16: *"Shepherd my sheep"* refers to the task of a hireling.
        v. 17: *"Tend my sheep"* refers to the full responsibility for the flock.
   C. A Review of a Shepherd's Heart: pages 13-22 in the text.
      a. A shepherd knows sheep have no sense of direction; they must be led.
      b. Size of a flock: no more than one shepherd can care for (15).
      c. Your task: to lead each person to discover and use their gifts.
      d. A shepherd doesn't *teach;* a shepherd *facilitates.*
      e. Let's look at the key points mentioned in these pages *(review of the contents).*

2. SHAPING YOUR MINISTRY
   A. Your personal ministry is covered in Part Two of the book.
   B. Your task is very precise: you are to equip the flock for ministry.
   C. This is to be done corporately and personally.
   D. Note the way your relationship is to be formed with each Cell Member:
      a. A *personal interview* is to be held with each incoming Cell member.
      b. Use of the *Journey Guide* must be mastered.

      c. Develop a prayer ministry which includes each person/family in the Cell.
  E. Create a "family" spirit among your flock members.
      a. Literally, your Cell is a "Basic Christian Community."
      b. The Cell is the first building block of the church.
  F. Goal: as quickly as possible, reach out to the lost.
      a. Never let Satan deceive you by thinking that you are a "closed Cell."
      b. Reaching the unreached should be the focal point for all you do.
  G. Children are not to be seen as a "bother."
      a. Don't make your children despise Cell meetings—see chapter 12.
      b. If you have children in your Cell, plan for them in what you do.

3. SHAPING YOUR CELL GROUP
  A. You'll want to refer to Section 3 in the book again and again as you learn to minister and facilitate in the cell group gatherings.
  B. Note the helps in chapters 15 and 16 related to special moments in the life of the group, and suggested "Ice Breakers."

4. SHAPING YOUR RECORD KEEPING
  • Each report form has been developed by cell leaders in the past, and have proven to be useful to them. You are free to use them, to photocopy them, and to revise them as needed.

3. OUTLINE: "HOW I PREPARE FOR MY CELL MEETING"

(Note: this is best presented by a seasoned cell leader who is respected by those attending the weekend.)

A FIVE STEP GUIDE
by Eugene Seow

Prayer: "Lord, make me an instrument,
An Instrument of worship.
I lift up my hands unto you."

STEP 1: PRAY AND PRAISE
　　　Prepare to live a *lifestyle* as you prepare for your ministry.

STEP 2: PRAY AND PREPARE
　　　Move towards a focus on the Cell members and their needs.

STEP 3: PRAY AND PRACTICE
　　　Practice, if necessary, for freedom in sharing the materials.

STEP 4: PRAY AND PRAY
　　　Listening to God for what the Cell needs from you is crucial.

STEP 5: PRAY AND PRAISE
　　　Give Thanks for the guidance the Lord provides you for your ministry.

15

SCHEDULE FOR YOUR CELL GROUP ASSIGNMENTS

You will be guided primarily by your Cell Leader during the next six months of internship. These will be some of the tasks you will experience:

Week 1: Cell Leader will review the meeting with you.
This will take place immediately after the cell meeting has concluded. (See page 248, Shepherd's Guidebook).

Week 2: You will lead the Ice Breaker.
This will be discussed with the Cell Leader in advance.

Week 3: You will lead Worship and the Lord's Supper.
This may be changed to another week by the Cell Leader.

Week 4: You will lead Edification Time.
This will be assigned to you and evaluated by the Cell Leader and even perhaps by the Zone Supervisor.

Week 5: You will complete a Cell Report; submit to Trainer.
This Cell Report should be a second copy for your use. Bring it to your Trainer for discussion and evaluation.

Week 6: You will lead "Share The Vision" Time.
This may involve your guiding the cell in a "round robin" of the John 3:16 diagram.

Week 7: You will visit a "Type A" unbeliever with a cell member.
This may involve taking a cell member who has just finished the John 3:16 Weekend to visit someone in his/her oikos.

Week 8: You will plan and Lead a Prayer Walk.
This may involve a special evening when the cell group substitutes this event for the regular meeting. The cell leader may assign to you the full charge of this event.

SCHEDULE FOR THE EIGHT TRAINING WEEKS

Your Trainer will spend most of the time in your training sessions providing you with experience in the areas of shepherding, management, and vision-casting. These ministry tasks are shown in the chart below. It may be revised by the trainer to accommodate your needs:

TRAINING DATES	SESSION	TASK	PRACTICAL ASSIGNMENTS — Trainer's Initial/Completion Date	READING ASSIGNMENTS — SHEPHERD'S GUIDEBOOK	Fellow Intern's Initial/Completion Date	ORDERING YOUR PRIVATE WORLD	Fellow Intern's Initial/Completion Date
	1	Nil	Nil	Chapt. 1-2		Preface to Chapt. 2	
	2	Lead Ice Breaker		Chapt. 3-4		Chapt. 3-5	
	3	Lead Worship & Lord's Supper		Chapt. 5-6		Chapt. 6-7	
	4	Complete a Cell Report, submitted to Trainer		Chapt. 7-8		Chapt. 8-9	
	5	Lead Share the Vision		Chapt. 9-10		Chapt. 10-11	
	6	Lead Edification Time		Chapt. 11-12		Chapt. 12-13	
	7	John 3:16 Visit		Chapt. 13-14		Chapt. 14	
	8	Plan & Lead a Prayer Walk		Chapt. 15-17		End Pages	

Note: Each Intern will have separate dates assigned for these class assigments.
Your trainer will give you the Dates and the Sessions for these tasks.

WEEK 1
CELL CHURCHES

CHAPTER CONTENTS

A. The Philosophy of Cell Groups

B. Cells in the Early Church

C. Cell Groups in Church History

D. Cell Groups in Today's World

E. In Cell Churches, Every Christian is a Minister

F. Overview of a Cell Church

G. The Structure that Serves the Cells

H. The Three "C's" of a Cell Church

I. Our Vision

J. Our Strategy

OBJECTIVES

1. Catch the vision that a cell church is a way to church growth.

2. Have an overview of what constitutes a cell church.

3. Know the difference between a church with cell groups and a cell group church.

4. Get an overview of the organizational structure of a cell church.

5. Understand the vision and strategy of a cell church.

A. The Philosophy of Cell Groups

The Biblical Foundation for the cell group concept presented in this course is based on the model used by the Lord Jesus Christ. His relationship with the apostles began on a one-to-one basis as He called them individually (Mark 3:13-14). The twelve then became a "cell group" for one another (Acts 1:12-14). Jesus then commissioned them collectively (Matthew 28:18-20) and no one was excluded from the command to reach the lost. A clear strategy was given: Jerusalem—Judea—Samaria—the ends of the earth (Acts 1:4,8). As the Holy Spirit filled the members in this first cell group, they started sharing their story (Acts 2:1-4, 15-21).

B. Cells in the Early Church

Cell groups were the model that the early church used resulting in the expansion of the church. Many people responded to the testimony of the apostles and were taken into fellowship as they met in one another's homes (Acts 2: 42; 46-47).

C. Cell Groups in Church History

As we look at church history, we find that the house church was actually the common structural expression of the Christian congregation.

When Constantine became a Christian, there was a move from underground worship in catacombs and house churches to cathedrals. The house churches which had been the symbol of community and spirituality disappeared from the mainstream of structural church life. However, parts of the monastic movement and "sectarian" groups continued to meet in house churches as a parallel tradition.

While the mainstream of the Reformation continued to be bound to the cathedrals, the Anabaptists, who had no church buildings, assembled in homes for worship and spiritual development. Next, the Pietists became the most definitive expression of the house church in the early Post-Reformation era.

The next important figure in church history, John Wesley, was profoundly influenced by the Moravians. His "holy clubs" became the basic structure for the Wesleyan Revival.

D. Cell Groups in Today's World

It is interesting to note that as we look around the world today, the churches which are experiencing phenomenal growth are all cell churches. This is caused by the powerful activity of the Holy Spirit, who is restoring the Bride of Christ to her first-century glory. Let us trace the contemporary scene of the global cell church movement:

Korea

Korea has a centuries-old commitment to Buddhism. Massive statues of Buddha are found throughout the land. Tens of thousands journey to mountain areas where shrines have been erected. A little over 100 years ago, the first missionaries arrived to evangelize this country. Although the Koreans responded to the Christian message, the harvest was slow. Then the cell church movement was used by Christ to invade the strongholds of paganism. The growth of cell churches in Korea has been breathtaking!

The largest local church in the history of Christianity exists in this land. It is the Yoido Full Gospel Central Church in Seoul, Korea. It has grown from a membership of five people who gathered in a tent in the slum called Sodaemon in 1958, to a congregation numbering 700,000 in 1995. The actual transition from traditional church life to cell life took place in 1964. The explosive growth continued nonstop from that point onward.

In a personal interview with Dr. Cho in 1984, he explained to Dr. Ralph Neighbour that he was seeking to curb the growth of the congregation by selecting capable men from the pastoral staff and giving them 5,000 members to launch new cell churches! The church's Prayer Mountain now registers over two and a half million people each year who go there to fast and pray. The time spent in prayer by this congregation exceeds any other single activity of their weekly schedule. Buses leave hourly from the central church building to carry cell members free of charge to this retreat site which has "prayer grottos" carved into the hillside.

If this church were the only cell congregation showing such growth in Seoul, it might be dismissed as the fruit of one dynamic pastor's personality, but this is not the case. There are dozens of other cell churches, nearly all growing at an amazing rate. Today, the world's two largest Presbyterian churches, along with the largest Methodist church, are cell congregations in Seoul. All are multiplying at a rate which far outstrips Korean churches which do not have a cell structure.

Seoul's skyline after dark is filled with neon crosses. Each cross indicates the existence of a church. There are literally thousands of such crosses! A Presbyterian pastor said to me, "Most of those crosses mark small churches with fewer than fifty members. They never seem to grow beyond that figure." Those who seek to discount the amazing growth of the cell churches in Korea must appreciate the fact that not all these churches are growing at the same rate. The difference is quite clear: In cell churches where all believers are equipped and involved in ministry, there is a phenomenally higher rate of church growth than that experienced by traditional churches, even in Seoul.

South Africa

Since 1993, South African churches have made a mass migration from the traditional forms of church life to the cell model. Pioneers like Hatfield Christian Church in Pretoria, which has had cells for years, have also revised earlier patterns of cell life to allow significant growth.

Over 200 churches have already completed *The Year of Transition* training provided by Touch International South Africa in 1995. The Apostolic Faith Mission has become the first denomination in the world to formally recommend to its hundreds of churches that the cell church model be adopted by all congregations. By 2005, it is forecast that South Africa will be the jewel of the cell church movement in all the earth.

Ivory Coast

Pastor Dion Robert launched the Yopougon Protestant Baptist Church and Mission in 1975. A few years later, he discovered the cell church principles and transitioned to a cell church structure. The twentieth anniversary of this church was celebrated in August, 1995, with over 80,000 members in the ministry. It has now planted daughter churches in Norway, Sweden, Denmark, France, the United States, as well as many African nations. This church has a huge complex with multi-story buildings and invites pastors from around the world to come to be trained in its school.

As with all other effective cell churches, several ingredients caused this church to grow rapidly. One ingredient is the amazing commitment to the vision of reaching the lost by the pastor. The second ingredient is the determination to make the cell the heart and soul of church life instead of using cells as "holding tanks" for Christians gathered through traditional building-based programs. A third ingredient is a theology that calls for complete surrender to the Lordship of Christ by all who enter cells. The final ingredient is a carefully developed organizational structure to minister to the cells. This includes outreach ministries performed by cell members, which put them in contact with many different groups within the community.

Dr. Ralph Neighbour, Jr., first visited this work during the Easter of 1988 as one of the preachers at the annual "Retreat" held in one of the largest stadiums in Abidjan. An estimated 35,000 people turned up for the five services held over three days. In preparation for the evangelistic harvesting event, the cells were divided in half to make room for the expected conversions. Ninety-nine per cent of those who attended were cell members and their guests which were unbelievers whom they had cultivated for weeks or months.

Thousands of conversions were recorded. The harvest was handled by carefully trained cell members who did all the counselling and enrolled the converts in cells.

This is a totally indigenous church which has none of the flavor of the influence of western missionaries. At the same time, it is uncanny to see the way it has developed a similar lifestyle to other cell churches situated on continents half a world away.

El Salvador

Mission Elim began in 1977 when Pastor Sergio Solorzano was called from Guatemala to begin a work in San Salvador with nine other brothers and sisters. Within seven years the church grew to 3,000 members using a traditional church structure. In 1985, Solorzano visited the Church Growth Conference in Seoul. Upon his return, he restructured all the work into a cell-based structure. There are now in excess of 120,000 members in the central church and additional cell churches planted in many other nations. This church has two cell meetings weekly—one for edification and the other for evangelism.

United States

The United States has been a laggard nation in transitioning into cell church structures. One reason for this is the independent spirit found in the American culture and its traditional church life, which rejects a lifestyle where people become accountable and responsible for one another. Another reason for the slow adoption has been the strong control over church life by rigid denominational structures whose churches are formed around doctrinal distinctions rather than around the "one another" accountability found in the New Testament church. Evangelism strategies have brought converts to the cross for freedom from the *penalty* of sin, without ever mentioning the place of the body of Christ, the cell group, as the place to come to find salvation from the *power* of sin. Most Americans place church life at the edge of their journey instead of in the heart of it. However, a dramatic shift is taking place at the present time within the United States, and there is a ground swell of transition taking place.

Emerging cell group churches using the TOUCH model are now springing up all over the nation. There are over 3,000 churches communicating with the offices of Touch Outreach Ministry in Houston and subscribing to *Cell Church* magazine. Some of them have started to greatly expand in size as transitions take place. In 1996, *The Year of Transition* will be available in areas of the U.S.A. and Canada.

Your training in this Cell Leader Intern course follows the strategy for equipping cell members developed first at West Memorial Baptist Church, Houston and further expanded by the devoted pastors and workers of the Faith Community Baptist Church in Singapore.

West Memorial in Houston is now pastored by Wallace Henley and has changed its name to the Encourager Church. It has set a goal of 50,000 people to be reached in Houston through its cell group network. It is to become a significant training base in future years for those who wish to learn how to pastor in a cell-based church.

In Shenandoah Valley, Virginia, there is a delightful model of a cell church which reaches across the farmland into several small towns with zones all linked together. Pastor Gerald Martin transitioned a traditional Mennonite church to become the Cornerstone Church and Ministries. This church expanded rapidly and now has a seminary for training pastors interested in the cell church.

In Portland, Oregon, New Hope Community Church will probably be remembered as one of the pioneers in cell group lifestyles. They form "Tender Loving Care Groups." Pastor Dale Galloway, who now teaches at Asbury Seminary, tells of the crucial decision he made to totally scrap the traditional form of the church several years ago. He had started out to blend the cell group church with the traditional structure used in the launch the work. Slowly, he realized he was trying to mix oil and water. He called in his staff and informed them their titles would change from "Minister of Education" and "Minister of Music" to "Zone Ministers." He rightly realized that it is not possible to have a church built around programs and build people at the same time! His model is one of several varieties found in the United States, and focuses on gathering people with special needs or interests into small groups. It is a "meta-hybrid" church, not a pure cell church.

Bethany Prayer Fellowship in Baker, Louisiana is a recent adopter of the cell church, using a hybrid structure adapted from the Faith Community Baptist Church in Singapore and the amazing cell church model formed by Pastor Solarzano in El Salvador. It is currently exploding with new growth and has constructed a "Touch Center" to house all of its District and Zone Pastors. It is closely linked to other churches around the nation who look to pastor Larry Stockstill for guidance.

Singapore

Pastor Lawrence Khong and the entire staff of Faith Community Baptist Church underwent a soul-searching process in 1987. The church had about 800 worshippers on 17 August 1986 and within six months, explosive growth was evident.

On the first anniversary the average attendance had climbed to 1,300. The major concern expressed by both the pastoral leadership and church members was the need for more personal pastoral care and maximum mobilization of all members. With this as a backdrop, and in consultation with Dr. Ralph W. Neighbour, Jr., the staff and core leadership of the church decided to restructure FCBC from a church *with* cells to a *cell church*. The growth to 7,000 in seven years has been a strong testimony to the value of a cell church strategy. One unique fact about this church is that it has pioneered in producing training materials for sister congregations who have chosen to build around the cell structure. The materials used in your training and many other TOUCH equipping materials were developed in the context of this body, now the largest Chinese church outside China.

Under the leadership of its District and Zone Pastors, the church staff trains its members in the *Touch Equipping Stations System*. It has planted work in Russia, Hong Kong, Taiwan, Kazakestan, China, Indonesia, the Philippines, and other areas within the "10/40 Window." It has also fraternally assisted sister churches in Singapore and Malaysia, hosting training events periodically for those from other nations in Asia and elsewhere.

Hong Kong

Pastor Ben Wong's Shepherd Community now embraces a consortium of other churches who have also reformed themselves into cell based structures. Together, these churches are bracing themselves for the 1997 takeover by China of the colony. At the writing of this book, eighty churches in Hong Kong have bonded together using cell groups. Pastor Wong's favorite statement about the joining of sister churches in the cell movement is to quote a Chinese proverb: "One hundred flowers bloom together!"

Ethiopia

When this nation fell to the communists, church doors were sealed and practicing worship of God was forbidden. Imprisonment and torture of church leaders was rampant. The Masorete Church, formed by Mennonite missionaries, went underground with 500 secret cell groups. Ten years later, they emerged with 50,000 believers! They is typical of "underground" cell churches meeting today in nations where churches are illegal.

Japan

Thanks to the Japan Church Growth Institute, several hundred pastors have launched the transition into cell church life. One Tokyo church, founded by David Yonggi Cho, now numbers thousands of members. Networks of other cell churches sponsored by cell pastors from Korea are emerging everywhere.

Commonwealth of Independent States

Cell churches are strong throughout the former Russian empire. Unreached people groups in Kazakestan have now been reached by powerful cell churches. Several in Almaty have grown to have hundreds of cells and have formed their own training schools. Moscow has, among other groups, the Moscow Christian Center, pastored by Jon Vande Reit, with cells spread all over the city. Many missionaries are presently planting cell churches all over the nation.

E. In Cell Churches, Every Christian is a Minister

The significance of cell churches has been downgraded because of the close alignment between cell churches and what is popularly called the "signs and wonders" movement. This is unfortunate. Those whose church life revolves around meetings held in a church building seem to have a limited vision of what is needed to bring the unreached to saving faith. When it is understood that *every Christian is a minister,* there is a major shift in how and where the power of God will be evidenced. His power will be experienced constantly as ministry is extended by cell groups to a broken people who are captives of Satan's deceptions.

The more one leaves the insulation of the traditional church environment, the more the need for the power of God to do the work of God is recognized. Physical, emotional and spiritual healing is constantly experienced by those in the cell church. Building up one another through using spiritual gifts is their lifestyle. Without the power of God, any ministry to the abused, the abandoned, and the possessed is a farce. Cell churches are not to be seen as Pentecostal or Charismatic, but as *Biblical.*

F. Overview of a Cell Church

1. The Cell: the "Basic Christian Community"

The cell is called the *Basic Christian Community*. The cell is the basic building block of the church. In other words, if there were only one "cell," there would be "church." However, unlike "house churches," a single cell does not stand alone. It is always connected to other cells to make up a regional "Congregation." Finally, all the cells in a community or region gather to worship God as the "Great Congregation" (see Psalm 68:26).

Each cell is led by a Cell Leader and an Assistant Cell Leader. Cells meet every week in one of the member's homes. They are not bound to one home, moving freely between homes. This helps to build a special bond between the members. Up to 5 cells clustered in a given locality are overseen by a *Zone Supervisor.* He or she is someone who has served effectively as a cell leader.

As a cell leader, you will literally become the pastor of up to 15 persons for a period of about six months. Every additional structure of this church exists *solely* to service life in the cells! Nothing is allowed to compete with the cell. All Bible study, prayer, equipping, fellowship, and ministry flows from the cells or is provided for them. Cells never grow larger than 15 people and multiply as they reach this figure. To repeat: *the cells are the basic building blocks of the church.* Every large-group activity involves the participation of cells. Hence, the combined strength of the cells is mobilized.

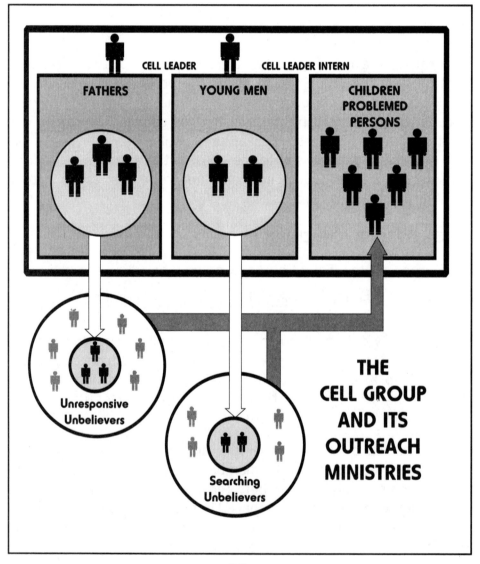

2. Two Types Of Cells:

A. For Nurture - the Home Cell

The Home Cell is the basic building block of the church. It is, in fact, a mini-church. In a cell, edification takes place as members care for one another, using spiritual gifts and support systems. Each cell is on a mission. It is constantly in touch with the unreached and is constantly ministering to them.

To repeat, the cell is the "Basic Christian Community." All members of the church are expected to function as a part of its ministry. It meets weekly and is always under the direction of the pastoral team of the church. Its life span before multiplication is typically about six months. The equipping of each believer is guided by a Cell Leader and the Cell Leader Intern. It is not just a "small group" in the church; instead, it is the focus of life for *every* believer, where edification and evangelism are practiced.

B. For Outreach - the Share Group

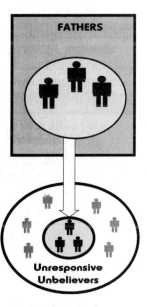

The Share Group is formed by three or four mature cell members, each ministering to two unbelievers. It is an evangelism extension of the cell, a "sub-community" for outreach. It meets separately from the cell for a single purpose: to connect believers to unbelievers who care little about spiritual matters. In a Share Group the unbelievers are impacted by the presence of Christ within the believers. Their interest in Christ comes alive as they are quickened by the Holy Spirit. They are led through a one-on-one study aimed at bringing them to Christ. They are then immersed into the life of the cell.

29

G. The Structure That Serves the Cells

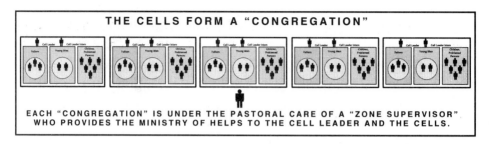

THE CELLS FORM A "CONGREGATION"

EACH "CONGREGATION" IS UNDER THE PASTORAL CARE OF A "ZONE SUPERVISOR" WHO PROVIDES THE MINISTRY OF HELPS TO THE CELL LEADER AND THE CELLS.

The congregation, or subzone, is a specific geographical area that includes one Zone Supervisor and three to five cells that relate together. Zone Supervisors are not paid by the church.

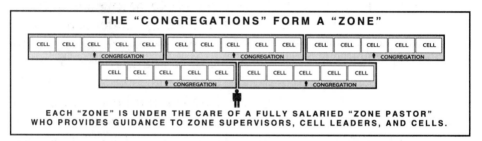

THE "CONGREGATIONS" FORM A "ZONE"

EACH "ZONE" IS UNDER THE CARE OF A FULLY SALARIED "ZONE PASTOR" WHO PROVIDES GUIDANCE TO ZONE SUPERVISORS, CELL LEADERS, AND CELLS.

The community is divided into a number of geographical areas termed Zones, or "Congregational Areas." Each congregational area has a resident area pastor who is employed by the church. Zone Pastors oversee from three to five Zone Supervisors and are responsible as co-ordinators for congregational activities, including leadership training and administration.

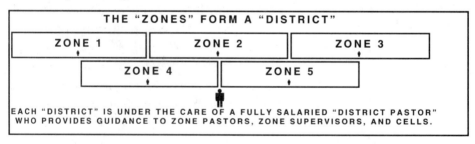

THE "ZONES" FORM A "DISTRICT"

EACH "DISTRICT" IS UNDER THE CARE OF A FULLY SALARIED "DISTRICT PASTOR" WHO PROVIDES GUIDANCE TO ZONE PASTORS, ZONE SUPERVISORS, AND CELLS.

The "Congregational Areas" are grouped into "Districts." Each district is overseen by a District Pastor who also serves on the Steering Committee of the church. He oversees up to five Zone Pastors and the congregational areas where he is resident.

H. The Three "C's" of a Cell Church

A cell church, therefore, comprises three basic components: *Cell, Congregation* and *Celebration*. The most important of the three is the *cell*. For those who are conditioned to think of the *congregation* as the focal point of church life, this will require a radical re-orientation.

1. Cell

Cells are the basic building blocks of all life forms. The cell is also the basic life form of the church. Participation in the cell church takes place by joining the cell. It is in the cell where people are nurtured, equipped to serve, and where members build up (edify) one another. The cell forms a community where believers are called to be accountable and totally transparent with one another.

While activities can be exciting and laughter can be good medicine for the soul, intimate friendships or the pouring out of one's heart does not and cannot happen in a large group. The cell meets this need. The key word here is kinship.

Edification is the primary activity of the cell. Each cell begins its sessions with a brief time of praise and worship. However, that is not its primary purpose. The Bible is used freely as a guide for its lifestyle, but the cell is not a place for Bible study. These needs are fulfilled at a different level in the life of the church. It is not necessary for the cell leader to be a great Bible teacher, or even a strong communicator. Instead, the cell leader must have a love for the flock and a desire to minister to their needs. He or she serves on a pastoral level, caring for the needs of the sheep. This pastoral ministry is directed by the Holy Spirit and is built upon Biblical teaching already received in a congregation or celebration assembly.

2. Congregation

A cell church member needs a circle of friends around him or her for fellowship. This is where congregational activities for groups of between 50 and 100 are organized. Large group interaction, mass teaching or information transfer takes place quite effectively here. The congregation may set aside a half-night for prayer, or sometimes several days for prayer. The congregational meetings or district meetings gather groups of cells together for special activities done throughout the year.

Here the cell leaders are equals with cell members, but loved and respected for their spiritual maturity as they provide direction for the less mature believers. The Zone Pastor is the person assigned a congregation of cells and ministers among them. He or she is gifted in counselling, administration and evangelism, but not in preaching or teaching. In no sense of the word does the Zone Pastor become the senior pastor of the cells and the congregation served. His or her ministry is people-oriented, not pulpit-oriented.

3. Celebration

The celebration is a mass gathering of every cell member in the church. It demonstrates their life together as they worship God. This city-wide gathering is used for praise and worship, solid Bible teaching, and evangelism. It is a vital part of the public witness of the people of God. There is no limit to the effective size. In fact, the slogan here is probably, "The more, the merrier!"

Celebration music focuses upon worship of the Godhead. There is much singing. The room is usually charged with joy. A full hour of praise is not unusual. Most cell churches must expand to two, four or even seven celebration services to accommodate all the people.

In addition, the celebration should always include the teaching of the scriptures with the cell group meeting in mind. The content of scripture is provided in the large group setting and is then processed in the cell group. It is important to understand that as you enter the ministry of a cell leader, *you are not to consider yourself the counterpart of a Sunday School teacher in a traditional church!* It is ill advised for you to repeat the teaching given in the celebration when your cell group meets. Your task is to *facilitate* the application of the biblical teaching by *providing a climate for edification.*

32

I. Our Vision

In the space below, write *from memory* the Vision Statement which has been prepared by your church:

_____

_____

_____

_____

_____

J. Our Strategy

In the space below, write the Strategy Statement which will now be explained by the Facilitator of this equipping session:

_____

_____

_____

_____

_____

_____

WEEK 2
THE CELL AGENDA

CHAPTER CONTENTS

A. The Cell Agenda

B. The Stages of a Cell Group

C. The Four Growth Phases of a Cell

D. Common Problems Encountered

E. Facilitator, or Teacher?

F. Exercising Spiritual Gifts

OBJECTIVES

1. Know the Cell Agenda.

2. Understand the stages the cell group goes through.

3. Anticipate the growth phases of a cell.

4. Understand some common problems in cell life.

5. Know how to be a facilitator.

6. Be able to incorporate spiritual gifts in the cell meeting.

A. The Cell Agenda

. . . let us consider how we may spur one another on toward love and good deeds. Let us not give up meeting together, as some are in the habit of doing, but let us encourage one another . . . (Hebrews 10:24-25)

These verses refer to the house meetings of the New Testament church, and help us to understand why they came together. This type of gathering was for fellowship, not for teaching. Perhaps the greatest deficiency among Christians in our day is the lack of heart-sharing and personal interaction. Cell groups provide a setting where there can be maximum sharing and encouragement of one another.

The cell agenda, in a nutshell, is to fulfill the greatest of all the commandments: "To love one another."
- To love one another *inside,* the cell must *minister* (edification).
- To love one another *outside,* the cell must *multiply* (evangelization).

In order to fulfill its agenda, a cell gathering should improve the interaction and openness in sharing among its members. Worship, Bible study and fellowship are secondary. Interaction and openness among cell members is crucial for the survival of the cell.

The cell is both inward looking and outward looking. It seeks to help each cell member grow into ministry. Most important of all, however, is the importance of the group being outward-looking as the bring Christ into the lives of unreached people.

Consider the gathering of the 120 after Jesus ascended to the Father. *What was their agenda?* Perhaps one of them went to Peter and said, "What are we to do here? Did Jesus give you any agenda for us?" Perhaps Peter replied, "The agenda is—*us!*" Not until they were all in one accord did anything further take place. It was then the Holy Spirit fell upon them with tongues of fire. That fire was the *shekina* glory of God seen by Moses in the burning bush. Christ was poured into their bodies, and their ministry flowed from that experience. In your cell group, loving one another will result in ministry to others.

35

B. The Stages of a Cell Group

STRUCTURE OF A CELL MEETING (BETWEEN 90 AND 120 MINS.)

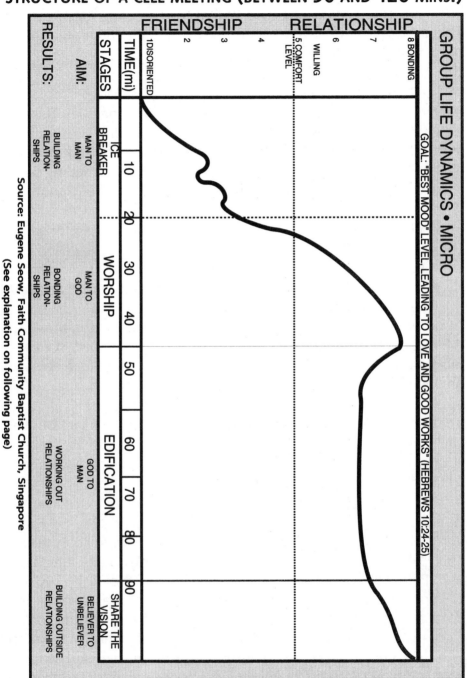

Source: Eugene Seow, Faith Community Baptist Church, Singapore
(See explanation on following page)

The graph on the previous page shows the importance of each of the four stages of a cell meeting. The success of each stage is dependent on how effectively the previous stage is handled.

The *Ice Breaker* raises the bonding level in the cell. The *Worship* will build from this level. The bonding level will flatten off slightly after the worship time to allow for *Edification* to take place. If the worship has been effective, edification will take place well above the comfort line. *Sharing The Vision* is the final stage of the cell. This stage is extremely important as it results in the bonding level in the cell reaching it's peak, and the very purpose of the cell being accomplished!

It is easy to remember these four stages by recalling the "Four W's":

    WELCOME: *Ice Breaker*
    WORSHIP: *Worship*
    WORD: *Edification*
    WORKS: *Sharing The Vision*

It is important that participants become involved in the cell group both socially and spiritually. The following suggested format is a good method of accomplishing this:

MEETING AGENDA	SPIRITUAL DYNAMICS	EMOTIONAL DYNAMICS	GROUP LIFE DYNAMICS
Welcome (Ice Breaker)	Man to Man *You to me*	Building Relationships	Get acquainted: History giving
Worship (Ministry)	Man to God *Us to God*	Bonding Relationships	Affirmation: Conflict Resolving
Word (Edification)	God to Man *God to us*	Working Out Relationships	Goal Setting: Community
Works (Vision)	Man to Man *God Through us*	Establishing New Relationships	Outreach: Multiply

STAGE 1: THE ICE BREAKER

During this initial stage light refreshments are served, so that, as the people arrive, they enter an informal, non-threatening environment. When the people have relaxed a little and are seated the leader asks some questions. This gives each one an opportunity to speak.

What Are Ice Breakers?

- Ice breakers are not games.
- They are activities that help people take the focus off themselves so they feel at ease with one another.
- They may require each person to say something on a predetermined topic.
- Or, small groups of twos or threes may be required to accomplish a task in a limited time.
- They bring everyone in the cell to a common focus.
- They help bind people together, usually on a superficial level.
- Do not expect too much from ice breakers.
- As the name suggests, they only break the initial hesitance of everyone present to speak openly.
- Ice breakers are not a waste of time, use them in every meeting.
- They are extremely valuable for cells where people are beginning to know each other, as well as for cells that have been together for a long time.
- They are only TOOLS to help members of a cell take the first step to enter into each other's lives after being absent from one another for several days.
- Ice breakers are able to focus the group as it meets.

ICE BREAKER

AIM: Interaction: You to Me

ACTIVITIES: Refreshments and Questions

ATMOSPHERE: Non-Threatening

DURATION: Approximately 15-20 Minutes

Watch for *crisis needs* during an ice breaker. It is not unusual for someone to signal they have a real hurt or problem during the ice breaker: "I heard this week that my mother has cancer." Obviously, you must return to minister to this need—but do not stop the circle of sharing. Say, "We've got to come back to you and share more about that, Susan. Thanks for telling us." Then, continue. This gives Susan a chance to form her comments, which may otherwise just "spill out" beyond what she feels comfortable sharing with the cell group.

The Quaker Questions

Quaker Questions have been used by hundreds of people to get acquainted with each other as an ice breaker. It is good to use them whenever a cell group is formed. They can be repeated each week a new person visits your group. None of the questions require disclosing intimate personal details. Each question should be answered by each person before the next question is introduced. Let each person in the circle answer in turn.

Serving as the facilitator, state the first question and then answer it yourself. Your answers will set the tone for all the rest. If you are brief, others will be brief. If you are long-winded, others will be too. Spend no more than one minute per person on each question.

- *Where did you live between the ages of 7 and 12, and how many brothers and sisters do you have?*

- *What kind of car did your family have?*

- *Who was the person closest to you?*

- *When did God become more than a word to you?*

STAGE 2: WORSHIP

This is an extremely important part of the meeting. The focus now moves away from the people and towards the Lord. The Body that has come together now recognizes the Head.

When this stage has been well planned and the leader is in touch with the Holy Spirit, the people will sense the presence and the power of the Lord. If there are no musicians in the group, taped music can be used or someone with a strong voice could lead without accompaniment.

WORSHIP

AIM: Interaction: Us to God

ACTIVITIES: Praise and Worship

ATMOSPHERE: Reverence and Thanksgiving

DURATION: Approximately **20** Minutes

STAGE 3: EDIFICATION

The focus now shifts to *the needs* of those present. Scripture will be used here, however, the Bible is a tool and is not to become the focal point.

The manifestation of spiritual gifts are vital during this time. Prayer will also form a large part of this stage in the meeting. As the people are encouraged and built up, ensure that all are participating.

EDIFICATION

AIM: Interaction God to Us.

ACTIVITIES: Spiritual Gifts and Encouragement

ATMOSPHERE: Dependence On the Holy Spirit
and Servanthood

DURATION: Approximately **40** minutes

If a topic is going to be discussed during this stage and there is no outline to guide you, here are some characteristics of a good topic;

- It should relate to things going on within your cell group.
- It should encourage, stimulate, or challenge.
- It should confront "fuzzy thinking" about values.
- It should be discovered by asking the group what topics they feel a need to discuss.
- It should become a "fire in your bones," that you are "on top of." It will have worked itself into reality in your own life and life-style.

STAGE 4: SHARE THE VISION

The focus of this part of the gathering is upon Christ's commission to us: we *all* have to reach the lost. The vision of the cell in its ministry to unbelievers is emphasized. As the cell members reach beyond themselves, the result is a sense of purpose and destiny.

SHARE THE VISION

AIM: Interaction: God through Us (Outside The Cell)

ACTIVITIES: Outreach Strategies Planned and Executed; Prayer Warfare Against Strongholds in the Lives of Unbelievers

ATMOSPHERE: Obedience to the Holy Spirit and Servanthood

DURATION: Approximately **10** Minutes

The purpose of each "Share The Vision" session is to discuss ways the cell and its individual members can create meaningful relationships with unbelievers.

During the first meeting of the cell group, the cell leader should have all the members write down the names of every unbeliever in their *oikoses*. These will include family members, neighbors, associates at

41

work, etc. These names should be turned in at the end of the evening and then copied by the cell leader. At the next meeting, the list is distributed to each cell member

The agenda for "Share The Vision" Times may include any of the following topics:

1. Discussion of the spiritual condition of unbelievers.
2. Planning for ways that the cell group can interface with unbelievers.
3. A "round robin" presentation of the *John 3:16 Diagram*. The cell leader takes a blank sheet of paper, writes the word "GOD" on the upper left corner, and passes it to the cell leader Intern, who explains what details about God should be drawn out from the unbeliever. The word "MAN" is then written, and the paper is passed on to the next person in the circle, etc. Those who have not yet attended the *John 3:16 Seminar* are asked to observe while the others share in this activity.

C. The Four Growth Phases of a Cell

Cell groups have a limited life. Long years of experience with groups has verified that they stagnate after a certain length of time. People initially draw from one another. After that, they tend to "coast" along together. For that reason, each cell group will profit from multiplying and developing new relationships after about six months.

Set multiplication as a goal for the group. Work toward that moment when your cell group "births" a daughter cell group. By the time this happens, you should have fully trained your assistant to become the new Cell Group Leader of this new group.

As a Cell Group Leader, you should also be selecting and training two or three of the cell members as potential cell leaders. The greatest tribute which can be paid to you as a Cell Group Leader is for your cell group to double and multiply itself into two groups. During the life of the cell, it will go through four growth phases. Be aware of them so you can minister effectively.

1. The Get-Acquainted Stage

First impressions are often based on past relationships with other people. Someone may say to you, "You aren't a bit like I thought you were when we first met!" This is a common reaction. It can take two or three sessions before cell group members overcome false impressions about each other. The get-acquainted process can be accelerated by taking the cell members on a weekend retreat, where you have concentrated time to spend with each other. It is also meaningful to sponsor a four to six hour activity on a weekend, such as a picnic with games, etc.

2. The Conflict Stage

When people finally understand each other, value systems will clash. One person may talk too much, making the cell group feel angry by this unwanted domination. Another person may be insensitive or someone else may be too sensitive. After four or five sessions together, these conflicts will surface in cell group discussions. A "sandpapering" effect will take place. People will then begin to trust each other enough to air their differences and to work through them.

You are encouraged to share with the cell *during a meeting* that conflict is a natural part of successful cell life. Gently guide the cell group, letting the participants share deeply. The members *will* resolve these differences. The result is dramatic! As you work through the conflict, the group's identity will be established, and a new commitment to the cell group will occur.

3. The Community Stage

The conflict stage is followed by a meaningful period in which the members move towards one another in a very special way. It is not only a period of enrichment—it is also a danger point! When the cell group has found meaningful relationships, it may decide it wants to close itself off, to remain undisturbed. If this is permitted, the cell group will turn into an ugly, selfish monster. As soon as you sense there is a strong bond built between the members, guide the group to reach out to others and focus on multiplication activities.

4. The Ministering-To-Others Stage

In the very first meeting, stress that the cell group exists to build up each member to help others. From the first session, every member should be encouraged to cultivate unbelievers. However, some of the members will not be ready to minister to others until the cell group reaches this fourth stage.

D. Common Problems Encountered in Home Groups

Many home groups have been started without a biblically based foundation. The following are some examples of common problems encountered in home groups not properly grounded:

PROBLEM	CHARACTERISTICS	BASIC FLAWS

"Self-centered" group	• A spirit of self-centeredness
	• Self-enrichment
	• No commitment to the group
	• When my need is met I will leave
	• Only reason for attending is to have my needs met
	• Purpose of this group is
	  • Bible study
	  • Personal crisis
	  • Special interest
		• Lack of servanthood

"Personal Enrichment" Group	• People endeavor to become totally transparent, believing this is the way to higher levels of spirituality and self awareness	• Maturity is not reached in the vacuum of a closed group. • The alienation of this group will result in stagnation and death. • Living things don't last long in a vacuum.
"Strengthening the Witnesses" Group	• Spends time healing battle wounds • Much prayer for each other • Prayer for the lost • Christians with a desire to witness as part of their lifestyle have formed a group to encourage each other in the witnessing battles.	• They are close to reality, but witness alone rather than two by two. • Limited in its goal of winning the lost. • Does not expose unbelievers to the witness of God's people building up one another.

PROBLEM	CHARACTERISTICS	BASIC FLAWS
"Football Team" Group	• Come together to plan strategy in much the same way as a football team would decide on tactics. • Set target groups (i.e. handing out tracts at a sporting event or beach evangelism during holidays). • These are teams of people who go on hospital, prison or team outreach.	• This form of evangelism does present a message, but it does not offer a community of love. We have more than a message to bring. We also have a lifestyle for people to embrace. The Body of Christ exhibits itself once again as being separated from the world around it.
"Bible Study" Group	• The leader follows an outline or section of Scripture or a topic is covered. • The group discusses the material. A commentary may be used as an aid.	• The group pools its mutual ignorance. • Someone with a teaching gift would end up giving a lecture.

E. How To Be A Facilitator

It is of vital importance that the cell leader be a *facilitator* and not a *teacher.* The difference between the two is:

- A *facilitator* provides *experiences* for the cell members.
- A *teacher* provides *knowledge* to the cell members.

The leader must prepare in advance for the cell group meeting. Using the outline supplied by the Zone Pastors, each aspect of the meeting needs to be prayerfully considered. A lack of preparation by the leader is inexcusable.

The effective facilitator will begin by creating proper physical surroundings. Cell group meetings can be demolished by any of these conditions:

- Great distances between the seats in the room.
- People like sitting ducks in a row, unable to see each other.
- People sitting behind other people, rather than in one circle.
- A telephone ringing every 10 minutes *(Take it off the hook!).*
- A dog or cat making the rounds of the cell group.
- A child that does the same, or who whines for attention.
- A vase of flowers or lamp obstructing the view of the members.
- A noisy TV or radio in an adjacent room.

1. The Four Parts of Facilitating

   a. Provide An Experience

In the place of a lecture or a teaching, let the group discover something by experiencing it. This is the purpose of small group life! The best way to accomplish teaching is by putting people in a room with all the chairs facing in the same direction. Teaching is a cognitive process. When you are meeting as a group, the emphasis should be on relational activity, which is why you sit in a circle.

   b. Get Feedback from the Group

In order to get feedback from the group, ask questions like:
   • What did you gain from this experience?
   • What new insights have we discovered?
   • What conclusions can we draw?

   c. Summarize the Group's Conclusions

This is actually for your benefit. Having your own biases colors what you think the group has said in the feedback time. Tell them what you think you heard them say, and correct any wrong conclusions immediately.

   d. Probe for Principles Retained by Group Members

Ask every cell member in turn, "What will you carry away from this experience?" This mutual sharing can sometimes trigger long and heartfelt discussions! You may see some of the most significant breakthroughs following this time of probing for principles learned.

2. Lessons in Facilitating from Our Lord

   a. He modeled His values as the disciples watched.
   b. He shared information in bits and pieces.
   c. He kept them in life situations, not in classrooms.
   d. He sent them out to try their skills.

e. He allowed them to make mistakes.
f. He let them learn from their peers.
g. He was patient when their values were wrong.
h. He waited for "teachable moments" to occur.
i. He used time as a shaping factor.
j. He used outside circumstances to impart truth.

F. Exercising Spiritual Gifts

Don't settle for gatherings where you have a polite time, a nice Bible study, or warm fuzzies in your emotions. Exercise the gifts the Lord has given you for the Body, and let them flow to edify others. When the Head begins to control the actions of the Body, throw away your notes and go with the flow.

> *"Now to each one the manifestation of the Spirit is given for the common good. To one there is given through the Spirit the message of wisdom, to another the message of knowledge by means of the same Spirit, to another faith by the same Spirit, to another gifts of healing by that one Spirit, to another miraculous powers, to another prophecy, to another distinguishing between spirits, to another speaking in different kinds of tongues, and to still another the interpretation of tongues. All these are the work of one and the same Spirit, and he gives them to each one, just as he determines. The body is a unit, though it is made up of many parts; and though all its parts are many, they form one body. So it is with Christ. For we were all baptized by one Spirit into one body—whether Jews or Greeks, slave or free—and we were all given the one Spirit to drink. Now the body is not made up of one part but of many. If the foot should say, "Because I am not a hand, I do not belong to the body,: it would not for that reason cease to be part of the body. And if the ear should say, "Because I am not an eye, I do not belong to the body," it would not for that reason cease to be part of the body...Now you are the body of Christ, and each one of you is part of it."(1 Corinthians 12:7–16, 27)*

Paul sees spiritual gifts distributed among us for the common good. Since I need your gift, and you need mine, we give and share equally with one another. When you meditate on this, it is the obvious result of our being made one Body!

1 Corinthians 14:23-25 points out that a special witness is given to the unbelievers as God's people manifest His presence and power:

> *But if an unbeliever or someone who does not understand (or, some inquirer) comes in while everybody is prophesying, he will be convicted by all that he is a sinner and will be judged by all, and the secrets of his heart will be laid bare. So he will fall down and worship God, exclaiming, "God is really among you!"* (1 Corinthians 14:24-25)

WEEK 3
WORSHIP IN THE CELL

CHAPTER CONTENTS

A. Definition of Praise

B. Definition of Worship

C. Praise and Worship in A Nutshell

D. The Different Postures of Praise and Worship

E. Functions of a Worship Leader

F. Guidelines in Leading Worship

G. Planning The Worship Session and Selection of Songs

H. Possible Framework (Example)

I. Celebrating The Lord's Supper

OBJECTIVES

1. Know the difference between praise and worship.

2. Know the different ways of worship as found in the Bible.

3. Know how to plan a 20-minute worship session that flows smoothly.

4. Release words of knowledge and prophecy during worship.

5. Learn how to encourage ministry in a cell meeting.

6. Know how to conduct the celebration of the Lord's Supper in a cell meeting meaningfully.

A. Definition of Praise

- Praise is adoration directed towards God or an expression to others about God.
- Praise is usually dynamic, vocal and often loud.
- Praise is being preoccupied with who God is and what He has done.
- Praise is energetic acclamation accompanied with singing, shouting, proclaiming, dancing, playing of musical instruments, and other external forms.
- Praise involves the emotions.
- Praise is a weapon for spiritual warfare (2 Chronicles 20:20-28).

B. Definition of Worship

- Worship means "to ascribe worth or value, or to count worthy;" that is, "to acknowledge that God is worthy."
- Worship is conversation between God and man. This is a dialogue that should go on constantly in the life of a Christian.
- Worship is giving to God our total self.
- Worship is the outcome of the fellowship of love between the Creator and man in response to God's love.
- Worship is one's expression of love, adoration and praise to God with an attitude which acknowledges His supremacy and lordship.
- Worship means "to feel in the heart."
- Worship is the ability to magnify God with our whole being—body, soul and spirit.
- The heart of worship is the unashamed pouring out of our inner self to the Lord Jesus Christ in affectionate devotion.
- Worship is extravagant love and communion with God that can only be experienced by His loved ones.
- Worship is usually intimate, involving communion and fellowship.

C. Praise and Worship Contrasted

Praise	Worship
Celebration	Contemplation and reflection
Loud	Still and quiet
Warfare	Wonder and Majesty
What He has done	Who He is
Receiving favor or things	Giving honor
God's command	Our willingness
Arises from seeing His acts	Arises from knowing Him
Happiness	Holiness and humility
Expresses "Thank You!"	Expresses "I Love You!"

D. The Different Postures of Praise and Worship

Meditate on these scriptures. They help us realize that in the cell group worship experience, all these postures are biblical:

1. The Laughing Mouth
   "Our mouths were filled with laughter, and our tongues with songs of joy." (Psalm 126:2)

2. The Singing Mouth
   "I will sing of the Lord's great love forever; with my mouth I will make your faithfulness known through all generations." (Psalm 89:1)
   "Sing to Him, sing praise to Him; tell of all His wonderful acts." (Psalm 105:2)

3. The Bended Knee
   "Come, let us bow down in worship, let us kneel before the Lord our Maker." (Psalm 95:6)

4. The Bowed Head
   " . . . Then they bowed down and worshiped the Lord with their faces to the ground." (Nehemiah 8:6)
   " . . . so they sang praises with gladness and bowed their heads and worshiped." (2 Chronicles 29:30)

5. The Clapping Hands
   "Clap your hands, all you nations; shout to God with cries of joy." (Psalm 47:1)

6. The Shouting Voice
   "Come let us sing for joy to the Lord; let us shout aloud to the Rock of our salvation." (Psalm 95:1)
   "Shout for joy to the Lord, all the earth, burst into jubilant song with music; make music to the Lord with the harp, with the harp and the sound of singing, with trumpets and the blast of the ram's horn—shout for joy before the Lord, the King." (Psalm 98:4-6)

7. The Lifted Hands
   "Let us lift up our hearts and our hands to God in heaven" (Lamentations 3:41)
   "Hear my cry for mercy as I call to you for help, as I lift up my hands towards your Most Holy Place." (Psalm 28:2)
   "Lift up your hands in the sanctuary and praise the Lord." (Psalm 134:2)

8. The Prostrated Face
   "When all the people saw this, they fell prostrate and cried" (1 Kings 18:39)
   "And the twenty-four elders, who were seated on their thrones before God, fell on their faces and worshiped God." (Revelation 11:16-17)

9. The Uplifted Head
   "Lift up your heads, O you gates; be lifted up, you ancient doors . . ." (Psalm 24:7)

10. The Dancing Body
    "Then Miriam the prophetess, Aaron's sister, took a tambourine in her hand, and all the women followed her, with tambourine and dancing." (Exodus 15:20)
    "David, wearing a linen ephod, danced before the Lord with all his might . . ." (2 Samuel 6:14)
    "Let them praise his name with dancing and make music to him with tambourine and harp." (Psalm 149:3)

E. Functions of a Worship Leader

1. To provide the best environment possible for the people to worship.
2. To bring focus and direction.
3. To encourage unity within a cell.

F. Guidelines in Leading Worship

1. Be a worshipper
   a. The Father seeks worshippers: *"Yet a time is coming and has come when the true worshippers will worship the Father in spirit and truth, for they are the kind of worshippers the Father seeks."* (John 4:23)
   b. Worshippers are givers.
   c. Worshippers carry with them the fragrance of Christ.
   d. Worship is an expression of love, adoration and praise to God with an attitude which acknowledges His Lordship.

2. Pray, Plan and Practice
   a. Plan for worship as you would plan for a Bible study.
   b. Pray and ask God for a focus or a theme.
   c. Pay attention to the atmosphere you want to achieve.
   d. Select songs to suit the theme.
   e. Meditate on God's Word, reflecting on the words of the songs.
   f. Rehearse all the songs you have chosen.
   g. Know how to link the different songs. It is usually more difficult to link fast songs because of the short pauses in between. If you are not sure how to flow in and out of each song, keep practicing until you get it right.
   h. Decide on the number of times you would like to sing each song.
   i. Plan a time for sharing an appropriate Scripture or releasing any words of encouragement that there may be.

2. During the Worship
   a. Lead by being observant and sensitive.
   b. Be in charge of the session. Even if you are unsure or nervous, do not tell the people.
   c. Focus on God and allow Him to lead you in His confidence.
   d. Be sensitive to the Spirit's promptings. Although you have prepared a certain format always allow the Spirit to lead you.
   e. Use an appropriate tempo to achieve and sustain an atmosphere of worship.
   f. Always expect God to be present.

3. Things to avoid when leading worship
   a. Avoid an impromptu selection of songs. Prepare beforehand.
   b. Avoid long introductions and unnecessary explanation or commenting between songs.
   c. Avoid choosing songs that the cell members do not know.
   d. Avoid linking songs in different keys.
   e. Don't insist on singing all the songs that you have prepared. Be sensitive to the flow of the Holy Spirit.

G. Planning The Worship Session and Selection of Songs

1. Plan to direct the focus to God.
2. Try to visualize the flow of the praise and worship that you have prepared.
3. Pray for wisdom and sensitivity to the guidance of the Holy Spirit.
4. Consider the theme of the cell meeting and co-ordinate with the cell leader.
5. Avoid sudden or drastic changes in tempo.
6. Choose songs with the same theme, and if possible a similar tempo.
7. A time of praise usually comes first, followed by worship at a slower tempo.

H. Possible Framework (Example)

Theme
> To acknowledge Christ as Lord and King and to offer ourselves afresh as a living sacrifice.

Scripture Passage (Optional)
> *"Therefore I urge you, brothers, in the view of God's mercy, to offer your bodies as living sacrifices, holy and pleasing to God—this is your spiritual act of worship."* *(Romans 12:1)*

Songs of Praise (10 mins) Key: D
1. Great and Mighty Is He
2. My life Is In You, Lord
3. I Will Sing of the Mercies of the Lord, Forever

Songs of Worship (10 mins) Key: F
4. I Love You, Lord
5. I Worship The Lord God Most High
   (Pray for God to manifest His presence. If appropriate, release any prophecies given to cell members.)
6. Come Into the heavenlies
7. Who is like unto Thee?
   (Encourage cell members to reaffirm the Lordship of Jesus in their lives. Release ministry and pray for the person next to you.)

I. Celebrating The Lord's Supper

1. Why we celebrate the Lord's Supper in the cell meeting:

Jesus died to justify and purify sinful men through His act of propitiation on the cross. The breaking of His body and the shedding of His blood made peace with God possible for mankind. It also made it possible for Him to indwell a pure, new body. He became the head of His Body at the Cross.

2. The Beauty of the Lord's Supper

   a. The Lord's Supper was precious to the early church from their very first gatherings because it was a constant reminder of the place and the cost of their birth and their life.

   b. The Lord's Supper is a community activity and therefore appropriate to share in a cell meeting.

   c. In the early church a common meal would begin with the breaking of bread and close with the passing of the cup. This followed the Passover tradition, which had been carried on for centuries. This was continued by the early church in remembrance of the death of Jesus. Thus, the "love feast" began and ended with a reminder that the life of the "ecclesia" ("called out ones") began at the cross.

3. Purpose of the Lord's Supper

   a. Remembering the Lord's death
"And when He had given thanks, He broke it and said, 'This is my Body, which is broken for you, do this in remembrance of me.' In the same way, after supper He took the cup, saying, 'This cup is the new covenant in my blood; do this whenever you drink it, in remembrance of me.'" (1 Corinthians 11:24-25)

   b. Receiving a special blessing from the Lord
"Is not the cup of blessing which we bless a sharing in the blood of Christ? Is not the bread which we break a sharing in the body of Christ? . . . You cannot drink the cup of the Lord and the cup of demons. You cannot partake of the table of the Lord and the table of demons." (1 Corinthians 10:16 and 21)
"Therefore, whoever eats the bread or drinks of the cup of the Lord in an unworthy manner will be guilty of sinning against the body and blood of the Lord." (1 Corinthians 11:27)

   c. Recognizing that we are one Body in Christ
"Is not the cup of blessing which we bless a sharing in the blood of Christ? Is not the bread which we break a sharing in the body of Christ? Since there is one bread, we who are many are one body; for we all partake of the one bread." (1 Corinthians 10:16-17)

   d. Declaring the death of Christ to the world
"For whenever you eat this bread and drink this cup, you proclaim the Lord's death until He comes." (1 Corinthians 11:26)

4. Preparation for the Lord's Supper
   a. Prepare one cup of grape juice.
   b. Prepare a piece of cracker for each person, or have a piece of bread from which fragments can be removed.
   c. Prepare a song or two to sing during the celebration. This could be incorporated into the worship time, preferably at the end.
   d. Prepare a passage to be read at the beginning to help members focus their thoughts.

5. Procedure for the Lord's Supper
   a. Proceed with the Lord's Supper after the worship or discussion.
   b. The leader can read 1 Corinthians 11:23-26:
"For I received from the Lord what I also passed on to you; the Lord Jesus, on the night He was betrayed, took bread, and when He had given thanks, He broke it and said, 'This is my body, which is for you; do this in remembrance of me.' In the same way, after supper He took the cup, saying, 'This cup is the new covenant in my blood; do this, whenever you drink it, in remembrance of me: For whenever you eat this bread and drink this cup, you proclaim the Lord's death until He comes.'"

   c. The leader can briefly explain as follows:
"We have come together to observe the Lord's Supper. As we partake of this bread and cup, we remember the death of the Lord for our sins and we receive a blessing from the Lord. I want to invite all who have personally accepted

Jesus Christ as Saviour to join us in this remembrance. If you have not accepted Jesus Christ as your Saviour, you may not partake of the bread and cup. However, we are so glad you are with us and we want to declare to you what the Lord has done for us. As we partake of this, we want to pray a blessing for your life, too."

d. The leader can ask one person to lead a prayer of thanksgiving for the bread and cup.

e. A piece of cracker or bread will be served to each cell member. A cup of juice will be passed around. *(Note: physicians indicate the possibility of germs being spread by sharing the common cup is negligible; a cloth can be used to wipe the rim between each person's use.)*

f. The cell members then bless each other with the bread and the cup.

WEEK 4
EDIFICATION IN THE CELL

CHAPTER CONTENTS

A. God's Relationship to Us

B. Why the First Century Church Met in the Temple and in Homes

C. The Basic Christian Community (Cell) is Different from a Modern Small Group

D. Why are Cells Successful?

E. Two Approaches to Cell Life

F. The Three Domains of Learning

G. Edification

H. Developing and Using Questions

OBJECTIVES

1. Understand that participation at cell and church-wide celebrations is important for growth.

2. Understand the basic nature and make-up of a cell.

3. Understand that the main factor in making a cell successful is Christ.

4. Learn how to develop questions that will encourage discussion during the edification time.

A. God's Relationship to Us

For this is what the high and lofty One says—he who lives forever, whose name is holy: "I live in a high and holy place, but also with him who is contrite and lowly in spirit, to revive the spirit of the lowly and to revive the heart of the contrite."
(Isaiah 57:15)

God lives in a high and holy place, but has also chosen to draw near to those who are humble and contrite. He could be described as the *most high* and the *most nigh* God.

The most high God is: **transcendent**
- above
- beyond
- eternal
- king
- sovereign
- holy

The church context for worshipping the Transcendent God is usually a *large group* setting.

The most nigh God is: **immanent**
- in the midst
- incarnate
- within
- abiding
- friend
- indwelling

The church context for worshipping the Immanent God is usually a *small group* setting.

B. Why The First Century Church Met in The Temple and in Homes

They met in the temple because the transcendent God of Abraham, Isaac and Jacob continued to meet them there. Temple worship, with its focus on the transcendent God, provided the first century Christians with the setting to worship the Most High God.

But the first century Christians also met in small home groups. Why? Two events help explain this: Firstly, in John 14, Jesus promised:
"I will not leave you as orphans, I will come to you."
"The Father and I will abide with you."
"The Spirit will be in you and with you."

The second event was at the moment of His death. At this time, the veil that enclosed the Holy of Holies, which symbolized the abiding presence of God, was torn in two from the top to the bottom. God moved His Holy of Holies to the place where two or three Christians gathered together in His Name.

The first century Christians met in small home groups because The Most Nigh God, Christ in their midst, met them there in a special way as He had promised.

These two settings of the New Testament church are not matters of convenience or culture but are expressions of the transcendent and immanent nature of God Himself.

C. The Basic Christian Community (Cell) Is Different from a Modern Small Group.

Examples of modern small groups would be *Alcoholics Anonymous* and *Parent Support Groups*, etc.

BASIC CHRISTIAN COMMUNITY	DIFFERENT IN . . .	TYPICAL MODERN GROUP
• The Church in nature, purpose and power	NATURE	• A small group that is an extension of the real church
• Every task fulfilled through the basic Christian community	FUNCTION	• The small group has a limited purpose
• Focus on the person of Christ	FOCUS	• Focus on performance for Christ
• Christ indwells and empowers	LIFE FORCE (DNA)	• The reason for success: techniques,method, materials, leadership
• Nurture, facilitate, shepherd	LEADERSHIP	• Teach, promote, motivate
• Transformation through relationships, love and body life	WITNESS	• Convince through information, logic and weight of argument

D. Why Are Cells Successful?

Jesus Himself is the one essential factor in the life of the cell.

> **"Christ in the midst" is the DNA of the cell.**
> **DNA:** deoxyribonucleic acid.
> "The blueprint; life force; genetic code; information;
> catalyst that tells the cell how to grow and what to do."

Jesus promised both to be present with His followers in His *ecclesia* (church) and to empower it. The nature of personal experiences within the cell change when He is the sole focal point. He begins to direct the cell as the Head, empower it with spiritual gifts and fill it with His power. Then, genuine edification and fellowship take place!

It is His presence that breathes life into the leadership, the music, the gifts, materials, Bible Study, fellowship and warm relationships. Jesus Himself is the one essential factor in the life of His called-out community on earth.

E. Two Approaches to Cell Life

The different approaches are epitomized by the biblical characters of Martha and Mary (Luke 10:38-42).

1. The Martha Approach: Performance

   - Perform a service for Christ
   - Do something for Christ
   - Expect others to help do something for Christ
   - Make something happen for Christ
   - Prepare for Christ's presence or coming
   - Work as hard as you can for Christ
   - Run everything smoothly for Christ
   - Co-ordinate Christ's schedule
   - Keep active when Christ is near
   - Get busy for the Lord to the point of distraction
   - See Christ in passing as you do your work
   - Complain to Christ about the service of others
   - Fulfill your duty even if relationships suffers
   - *Focus most of all on what is necessary (secondary).*

2. The Mary Approach: Person

- Enter into Christ's presence
- Sit at Christ's feet
- Look into Christ's face
- Listen to Christ's voice
- Receive Christ's power
- Expect Christ's healing from all hurts
- Lay all your cares upon Christ
- Feel Christ's gentle touch
- Know Christ's unconditional acceptance
- Rest in Christ's love
- Be a child in Christ's arms
- Enjoy Christ's safety
- Enjoy Christ's freedom
- Release all fear to Christ
- Wash Christ's feet (John 12:1-8)
- Do Christ's will from an overflow of His presence
- *Focuses first of all on what is better (primary).*

F. The Three Domains of Learning

COGNITIVE (KNOWLEDGE)	EFFECTIVE (VALUES)	PSYCHOMOTOR (SKILLS)
Requires a Teacher	Uses a Facilitator	Requires a Coach
Logic	No Logic	Repetition
Deals With Knowledge	Deals With Values	Deals With Skills
Classroom Theory	Experience	Practice

LEARNING PROCESSES WITHIN A CELL

In all cell learning situations, all three domains of learning are at work. However, it is important that leaders do not focus solely on the cognitive and the psychomotor domains. Of course, we need knowledge, especially that found in the Bible. We need to develop skills—like how to pray, how to share John 3:16, how to interact with an unbeliever, etc, as well.

However, the most important focus in cell life should be on the value changes arising from knowledge and skills acquisition. Now that we know God loves us, how do we respond to Him? Now that we know how to share John 3:16, what can we do with this newly acquired skill? How should it change our lives? As leaders in cells, it is our responsibility to help our cell members move beyond simply acquiring knowledge or skills to *living them out.*

A learned principle has to be changed into an experience. This experience must be tested against the principle before it is assimilated as a new value.

For example, God promises that He answers prayers. As a new believer, it is difficult to believe this principle. Therefore, it has to be tested.

The new believer makes a simple prayer request. Then, he experiences the answer. He recalls what the Bible says about God answering prayers. He then concludes that God does answer prayers. It gives him more confidence to pray more. As the years go by, this principle will become ingrained as a life value.

G. Edification

WHAT KIND OF "EDIFICATION FACTOR" ARE YOU?
(ROMANS 15:1–3)

Negative Factor in Edification

You attend the group with the expectation that your own pains, hurts, needs and problems must be solved by the group. you are bringing your ministry needs to the group and not to Christ. you "play your record" at every meeting.

Neutral Factor in Edification

You come to the group in spiritual neutrality, waiting for God or someone in the group to make edification happen. You are not offering yourself to Christ as an instrument through which He edifies the group.

Positive Factor in Edification

You come to the group prepared to be a positive force for God to use for edifying the group. Your purpose for being in the group is to be part of Christ's edification process for the group, not to receive some personal ministry.

The more negative and neutral factors at work in a group, the more human distractions and fleshly activities become the focus of what happens in the cell.

The more positive edification factors at work in the members of the cell the more Christ can edify and minister to the hurts, pains, needs and problems in the group.

1. Leading an Edification Time

   - Have an attitude of being an edifier.
   - Allow the edification time to flow into the time of worship.
   - Application of the sermon is the focus.
   - Facilitate, don't teach.
   - Be personal, specific and practical.
   - Lead into ministry.

2. Edification Time Overview

   a. Each person in a cell must learn to become an edifier, actually using spiritual gifts to build up the body. (1 Corinthians 14:26)
   b. Flow into edification from the worship time. Close the worship time by praying for the edification time.
   c. The focus may be on the application of the Scripture passage preached in the previous Sunday's service.
   d. You must facilitate, not teach. Teaching is the leader doing all the talking, facilitating is the leader getting the people to talk.
   e. Facilitate the discussion and sharing by leading the people to applications that are:
      - Personal
      - Specific
      - Practical
   f. Discussion and sharing should lead to a time of ministry through prayer and the exercising of spiritual gifts.

3. Preparation
   The cell leader must spend time listening to God and asking for direction before leading a meeting. Spend time praying daily for all cell members and the cell meeting.

4. Procedures
   a. Read the Scripture passage for the sermon.
   b. Ask questions which lead into the discussion. Focus on the application. If the cell members have difficulty being open, break into smaller groups of three or four of the same sex to talk.
   c. Gather everyone together for the summary. Close the session by praying for each other.

H. Developing and Using Questions

Asking good questions is a skill that takes time to develop. This skill requires practice. The more you use it, evaluate it and develop it, the better you will become at it.

As a cell leader, you will have many opportunities to grow in this area. The following are some basic guidelines to help you ask questions that will stimulate thinking and discussion. Work on it with the help of the cell members.

1. Discovery Questions

These are questions that help the group recapture the basic outline of the message. Examples of discovery questions are:

"What in this passage speaks to a condition you face?"
"What challenge do you sense God giving you in light of what we have discussed?"

Seek to state the points of the sermon in simple, timeless principles. This will enable a newcomer to participate. He or she can make simple applications in line with timeless biblical principles.

2. Understanding Questions

There are questions which help the group come to a greater understanding of the points mentioned in the sermon. An example of an understanding question is:

"Do you have any new insights into this passage, topic or point?"

Stay within the interpretation of the sermon. Do not discuss any disagreements on points made in the message, or start an argument. There probably will only be one or two persons in the cell who will consistently have this problem. Suggest discussing controversial points outside the cell meeting to prevent other cell members from becoming confused. Flow along with what is taught. Inform your zone supervisor regarding any problems.

3. Application Questions

The main focus of the discussion should be on these questions. Each person must be encouraged to share. At this point, you may decide to break the cell into groups of two or three and get them to share with each other on a more personal level. However, do not have too much moving around. Ask each person to turn to the nearest person and share. If the group is able to share openly, go around and have each person share his or her response.

The leader needs to move into the background at this time and allow the Holy Spirit to guide each person to share openly. Try to release ministry in the light of the sharing. The leader needs to be alert to notice obvious needs which may need ministry. Examples of application questions are:

"Of the three or four points in the sermon, which one most touched your life?"
"What is one area in your life God is telling you to work on?"
"Share a struggle in your life which God has brought to the surface because of Sunday's sermon?"
"Share a new insight which you have learned and would like to see in your life."

4. Questions to Facilitate Discussion

During edification time, it is important that the leader guard against preaching a mini-sermon. Try not to provide the answers to the questions asked. Be patient and wait for the cell members to talk. Try not to ask right or wrong questions. Should a member misread your question and answer out of context, do not tell him or her the answer is wrong. Instead, tactfully overlook it, asking more leading questions to guide the group to the right answer. You might also direct the question to someone else.

5. Some Tips to Remember When Forming Questions

Teachers know that the best way to ask a good question is to know the answer in advance! Start by writing out the answer you want. Then write the question to get that particular answer. If you do not get the answer you want when you actually ask it, try improving the way you word the question. In your daily life, make it a habit to ask questions. It's the best way to learn how to do so effectively.

WEEK 5
STAGES IN CELL GROUP LIFE

CHAPTER CONTENTS

A. What Was Early Christianity Like?

B. The Four Purposes of a Cell

C. The Life Cycle of a Cell

D. Strategies for the Different Stages in Cell Life

OBJECTIVES

1. Understand the purpose of a cell group.

2. Have an overview of the stages in the life span of a cell.

3. Understand the importance of multiplication in cell life.

4. Learn the dynamics of keeping a cell group alive.

A. What Was Early Christianity Like?

It is hard for us to visualize early Christianity. Certainly it was very different from the Christianity we experience in our culture today. Consider these differences:

- *There were no fine buildings . . .*
- *No hierarchy . . .*
- *No theological seminaries . . .*
- *No Christian colleges . . .*
- *No Sunday Schools . . .*
- *No choirs . . .*

—Only small groups of believers. . . small fellowships.

In the beginning there wasn't even a New Testament. The New Testament itself was not so much a cause of these fellowships as a result of them. Thus, the first books of the New Testament were the letters written to the little fellowships partly because of their difficulties, dangers, and temptations.

All that they had was the fellowship; nothing else; no standing; no prestige; no honor.

The early Christians were not people of standing, but they had a secret power among them, and the secret power resulted from the way in which they were members one of another.
                    —Elton Trueblood, The Yoke of Christ, page 25.

1. Changes in the church when it moved from the home to a Building:

THE LORD'S SUPPER—changed from symbolic to ritualistic
WORSHIP—changed from participation to speculation
WITNESS—changed from relationship to salesmanship
MINISTRY—changed from personal to social
DISCIPLESHIP—changed from apprenticeship to classroom training
FELLOWSHIP—changed from in-depth to superficiality
USE OF GIFTS—changed from edifying to impressing
STEWARDSHIP—changed from gift of the heart to dues

2. The New Testament model:

"God's household, which is the church of the living God . . ."
(1 Timothy 3:15)
"All of these must be done for the strengthening of the church . . . " (1 Corinthians 14:26)
"Speak to one another with psalms, hymns and spiritual songs. Sing and make music in your heart to the Lord. " (Ephesians 5:19)
"Let us consider how we may spur one another on toward love and good deeds... let us encourage one another. "
(Hebrews 10:24-25)

B. The Four Purposes of a Cell

1. Evangelism

The cell is the vehicle for body evangelism and the incorporation of new Christians into the body. It is a place to cultivate the fruit of evangelism. It provides fellowship, follow-up and nurture for new Christians. It is a place where the unsaved person is given the opportunity to see God's work in the lives of believers.

2. Edification

The cell has a non-threatening environment for spiritual growth. It is a place to build strong bonds of Christian Fellowship and is also a place for accountability. Here one finds a listening ear, prayer support and counsel. However, in order to experience body life, the cell member must come with the attitude of: "Lord, give me something to use to bless others. "

3. Effective Ministry

The cell is a place to equip the saints for the work of the ministry. It provides a place for spiritual gifts to be discovered and encouraged. There are unlimited opportunities for meaningful service in the cell which a traditional church structure is unable to provide. A cell lives out the Biblical principle that everyone is a minister.

4. Expansion of Leadership Base

The cell is the base for the selection, training and mobilization of leaders. Within the cells, leaders are launched into ministry.

C. The Life Cycle of a Cell

CHANGING FOCUS	STAGES IN CELL LIFE	DEVELOPMENT PHASE
TOWARDS THE GROUP Members focus on the idea of a cell	**Exploration/Honeymoon Stage**	PHASE 1: Birth and Infancy (Forming)
TOWARDS SELF Members focus on what the cell can do for them	**Transition/Conflict Stage**	PHASE 2: Childhood (Norming)
TOWARDS CHRIST Members lay down personal needs and focus on Christ	**Action/Community Stage**	PHASE 3: Teenage (Conforming)
TOWARDS THE LOST Christ turns the attention of the cell outward	**Ministry/Outreach Stage**	PHASE 4: Maturity (Performing)
TOWARDS GROWTH The cell now experiences cell multiplication	**Termination/Closure Stage**	PHASE 5: Old Age and Demise (Reforming)

1. Exploration Stage

During this stage, the cell member evaluates if he/she feels a sense of belonging to the cell in three areas:
   a. People:
      • Do I feel included in this cell?
      • Do I want to let the others into my life?
      • Can I trust the others enough to risk expressing my true thoughts and feelings?
   b. Power:
      • Will I be included in the decision-making process of the cell?
      • Will my ideas be included in the discussion?
   c. Purpose:
      • How will the cell use its time?
      • What kind of commitments will the cell ask me to make?
      • Will the cell meet my personal needs?

2. Transition Stage

This is the conflict stage of group life. Some questions that the group members will ask are:
- "Why can't we talk about something more personal?"
- "Who is really making the decisions?"

a. People:
- They must know, and be known by each other.
- They must feel that the leader cares for and respect, them.

b. Power:
- Members want to have some say in what the cell does.
- They want to know how decisions are made and to have more influence in the cell.
- The goal is to develop a sense of belonging.

c. Purpose:
- The purpose of the cell takes center stage.
- Many of the goals set for the cell will be questioned.

3. Action Stage

The key word here is freedom! Members become free to be themselves, to commit themselves to the cell and to talk openly. This is the time when the cell will accomplish most of its outreach in mission and evangelism.

4. Ministry Stage

This is the time when cell members begin to look beyond themselves to the world. It is a stage of wanting to share the experiences they have in the cell with others. This is also the time when they see the results of their effort in evangelism.

5. Termination Stage

Generally, the life span of any cell should be between six and nine months. We have learned that any cell which does not multiply after about 12 months will usually stagnate, lose its life or vitality, and eventually die. Every cell should have an ending of some sort, and each member should realize this from the beginning. Multiplication is a time of celebration. The leader must help to make multiplication a pleasant occasion for everyone.

Experience reveals that any cell which lives beyond 12 months usually exists without a mission or purpose. After this length of time, if no growth has been seen there will be a "spiritual funeral." The cell is buried.

D. Strategies for the Different Stages in Cell Life

STAGES	STRATEGIES
EXPLORATION	• It takes about three weeks for relationships to form. • Use the first session to get acquainted. • Use the second session to strengthen relationships. • Use 10 minutes or so in the rest of the meetings for ice-breaking. Do not start ice-breakers until all have arrived. Each ice-breaker is designed to permit each person to make an initial contribution. • Ice breakers should allow for history giving, affirmations, etc. • Focus on being friendly and common interests. • Share testimonies. • Share benefits derived from cell participation.
TRANSITION	• Assign responsibilities to core members. • All members evaluate the cell. • Discuss problems and projects together. • Leaders should try to talk less. • Evaluate members for potential cell leaders.
ACTION	• Train the members in personal evangelism. • Challenge them to memorize verses. • Strengthen the Sponsor-Sponsee relationship. • Bring them out for ministry, e.g. hospital or home visitations, interest groups, evangelism parties, ministry on Sundays, etc.
MINISTRY	• Encourage members to make interaction with unbelievers as a way of life. • Share the results of the ministry during cell meetings to encourage them to keep moving out. • This is a stage of exponential growth.
TERMINATION	• Make this time as pleasant as possible. • Tell cell members of this stage as early as possible so that they will not feel negative about it. • Make it a time of celebration.

ELEMENTS IN AN EFFECTIVE CELL ENVIRONMENT.

1. Love and acceptance.
2. Safety and comfort.
3. Empathy and comfort.
4. Hope and encouragement.
5. Power and control (authority and accountability).
6. Openness and honesty.
7. Freedom of expression.
8. Information about how to minister to others.

FUNCTIONAL HEALTHY CELL

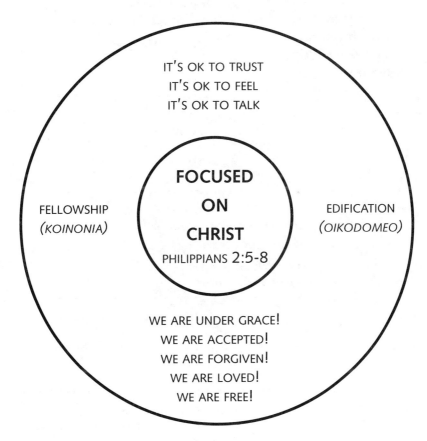

IT'S OK TO TRUST
IT'S OK TO FEEL
IT'S OK TO TALK

FELLOWSHIP
(KOINONIA)

**FOCUSED
ON
CHRIST**
PHILIPPIANS 2:5-8

EDIFICATION
(OIKODOMEO)

WE ARE UNDER GRACE!
WE ARE ACCEPTED!
WE ARE FORGIVEN!
WE ARE LOVED!
WE ARE FREE!

Source: Bill Beckham

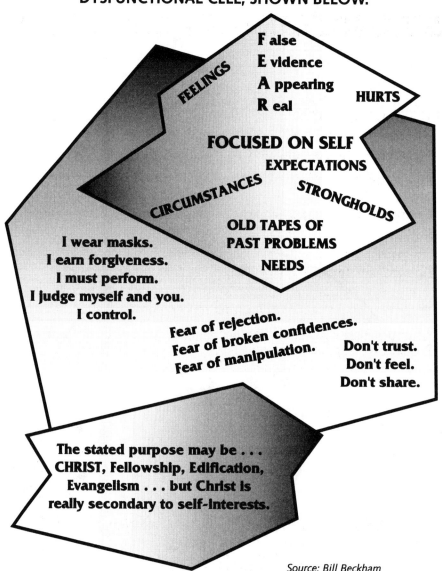

F alse
E vidence
A ppearing
R eal

FEELINGS

HURTS

FOCUSED ON SELF

EXPECTATIONS

CIRCUMSTANCES

STRONGHOLDS

OLD TAPES OF
PAST PROBLEMS

NEEDS

I wear masks.
I earn forgiveness.
I must perform.
I judge myself and you.
I control.

Fear of rejection.
Fear of broken confidences.
Fear of manipulation.

Don't trust.
Don't feel.
Don't share.

The stated purpose may be . . .
CHRIST, Fellowship, Edification,
Evangelism . . . but Christ is
really secondary to self-interests.

Source: Bill Beckham

WEEK 6
EVANGELISM IN CELL LIFE

CHAPTER CONTENTS

A. Evangelism in Cell Life is Essential for the Continual Growth of the Cell

B. Evangelism Is the Result of *Oikos* Penetration and Relationship Building

C. Evangelism Takes Place Through the Cell

D. Tools to Share the Gospel with Unbelievers

E. Procedures for Conducting "Share The Vision" Times

OBJECTIVES

1. Emphasize evangelism as an essential aspect for the growth of the cell.

2. Know that evangelism should be a result of *oikos* penetration and relationship building.

3. Establish whether or not a cell has all the elements for successful evangelism.

A. Evangelism in Cell Life Is Essential for The Continual Growth of the Cell

1. The Harvesting System

James F. Engel and H. Wilbert Norton in their classic book on Christian communication, *What's Gone Wrong With the Harvest,* conclude that the church no longer has cutting blades that can harvest. They state that the cutting edge of any Christian organization should be "a research-based, Spirit-led strategy to reach people with the Good News and to build them up in faith."

In the traditional Program Base Design Church, the "cutting blades" are nothing more than a strategy to mobilize the programs of that church, often resulting in the insertion of parachurch organizations, evangelism committees, one-night visitation programs, and mission boards.

The first Century church didn't think a lot about strategies or evangelism programs. The design of the church was to form Basic Christian Communities (cell groups) which was the harvesting system of the church. Without this kind of system, the cutting blades, no matter how sharp or polished, will be ineffective.

2. An Effective Harvesting System Must Provide:

- A context near enough to the harvest to provide co-ordination and support.

- A trained work force that is strategically positioned with an attitude of wanting to harvest.

- A source of power and energy that runs the harvesting machinery.

- Adequate periods of time available to do the harvesting.

- Necessary support equipment on hand.

- Cutting blades that can actually do the harvesting.

Operating through cell groups, the cell church is designed by Christ to do all these things:

- The cell church lives on the cutting edge of the harvest.

- It has a work force on site, ready to harvest.

- It trains its workers out in the fields to become leaders and coordinators.

- All equipment, tools and resources are available in the cell itself.

- Functioning as the Body of Christ, the small communities tap into the source of spiritual power.

- Activities are streamlined so that there is time to harvest during daily living.

The cell group must be a place of evangelism. Think of the cell group as a church with unsaved people all around it. Some will come once in a while. Others will be in the *oikos* of all the cell members. Hence the group must be very mindful of evangelism as one of the pillars in cell life.

In the past, evangelism conjured up the image of Christians distributing tracts in a busy, crowded shopping district or approaching strangers in a park to talk about the Gospel, or even bringing friends or colleagues to big evangelistic meetings organized by different churches. We seemed to portray the image of a "tiger" stalking its prey, waiting for the right time to pounce on the unbeliever to talk about the Gospel.

B. Evangelism Is The Result of *Oikos* **Penetration and Relationship Building**

1. Characteristics of Evangelism

   a. Evangelism is a process.
   b. Evangelism takes time.
   c. Evangelism works through relationships.
   d. Evangelism involves teamwork *(1 Corinthians 3:6)*.
   e. Don't bruise fruit which is meant to be picked by another.

THE RESPONSE PYRAMID

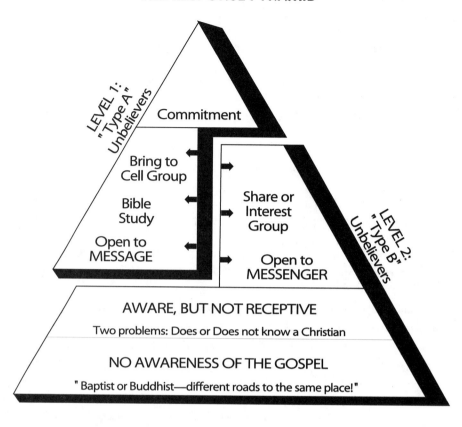

Evangelism in the cell is relational. With reference to the response pyramid, we need to be aware that unbelievers are at different levels of responsiveness. Only unbelievers who are near the top of the pyramid will respond positively to the distribution of tracts, evangelistic meetings, etc. The majority of unbelievers do not belong to level 1 or 2 on the pyramid. Therefore, they will be turned off if we are too trigger-happy in persuading them to become Christians.

We must first develop relationships with them. We must be completely genuine in knowing them as people, irrespective of whether they want to talk about God or not. We must be extremely natural in talking about God's goodness in our lives. They will not accuse us of trying to convert them if we constantly tell them of the answered prayers and miracles in our lives. One day, they will ask about this God we talk so much about. That's the time to share John 3:16 and your testimony.

Make mention of these unbeliever friends in your cell meetings. Encourage your sponsor and sponsee, or even all the cell members, to pray for them daily. God will answer these prayers. It's powerful, if evangelism is shared in the community.

2. *Oikos* Connections—The Bridge to the Unbeliever

"Oikos" refers to one's "primary group." This Greek word is found repeatedly in the New Testament, and is usually translated "household." However, it doesn't just refer to family members. Every one of us have a "primary group" of friends who relate directly to us through family, work, recreation, hobbies, and neighbors. These are the persons we talk to, relate to and share with, for at least a total of one hour each week.

We may know as many as two hundred people by name, and may have occasional relationships with several dozen. However, it is unusual to find a person who has as many as twenty people in their *oikos,* or primary group. A recent survey of Christians revealed they average about nine such people, and a large percentage of them had not developed a new *oikos* relationship in six months.

Life is made up of endless chains of *oikos* connections. Every person in your cell is already entwined in these relationships. Newcomers feel very much "outside" when they visit your group for the first time, unless they have established an *oikos* connection with a cell member. If they are not "kinned" by the members, they will not stay very long or try very hard to be included before they return to their old friends.

The size of an *oikos* depends on the capacity of a person to carry on relationships with others. Those who have been deeply scarred emotionally may have only three to five people in their *oikos,* while those with unstressed past lives will have larger ones. Sadly, those who most need love and friendship are those with the least opportunity to receive it. Each person lives within the primary group, and is strongly influenced by it. One of your tasks as a cell leader is to sensitize your cell members to the unbelievers in their *oikoses*.

3. The *Oikos* Strategy

What happens when a Type "A" unbeliever comes to a Celebration? A cell member, using *Touching Hearts Guidebook*, has been trained to make contact on behalf of the cell. A special relationship develops between the visitor and the visited. In the proper way, a friend asks a friend about his relationship with the Lord. The person shares that the issue has never been settled. Using John 3:16 and a simple drawing which can be done on the back of a place mat in a restaurant, a two way discussion takes place about the meaning of becoming a believer. The seeker fully realizes what it means to declare Christ as Lord, and then accepts Christ. He begins immediately to mature through attending the cell.

The family of this new convert, along with friends and business contacts, is his *oikos*. The cell member who brought him to Christ meets most of them when introduced by the new convert and is therefore accepted into the "inner circle" of the group.

Luke 10:5-6 tells us when we enter an *oikos*, we are to first say, "Peace to this *oikos*." If a "man of peace" *(someone searching for peace)* is there, your peace *(that's Jesus—He is our peace!)* will rest on him. If not, it will return to you.

Here's the strategy the cell members use to journey into new territory where they have not had previous contacts. They are to find a person who will bring them into their *oikos*.

They are to specialize in penetrating *oikoses*! No suggestion is made of their doing "personal evangelism." Stress is to be placed upon this point: their peace is to be offered not just to the first person they meet who belongs to an *oikos*, but to *every person* within it. They are "fishing" for a special type of person, called "a man of peace."

82

This harvest principle must not be ignored any longer! The initial contact with anyone should first be seen as a credential to meet an *oikos* of people, to live in their community of life, and to find the key person who is willing to receive the peace of salvation. Thus, cell group outreach is always to be seen as coming *from* the household of faith *to* those households who live in despair. For that reason, penetration is to be done by at least two believers from the cell group. Together, they model the love and fellowship which binds them together through the *oikodomeo* experiences they have had in their cell group in previous weeks. It's literally bringing the Kingdom of Christ into the kingdom of satan.

4. The Same Pattern Works With Type "B" Unbelievers

Without faith bridges to cross over into an *oikos*, there must be another step before the hard core unbeliever will be responsive. Such people are intensely driven by their own desires, and are best reached by "scratching where they itch." This is where the Share Group has proved to be powerfully effective.

C. Evangelism Takes Place Through the Cell

The cell is to be a place of evangelism. Think of the cell as a witness point with unsaved people all around it. Some unbelievers will attend special fellowship times held by the cell. Others will be in the *oikos* of a cell member. Therefore, the individuals in each cell must be mindful that evangelism is one of the pillars in cell life.

Members should constantly share about their contacts with unbelievers during the cell meeting. As you recall, the cell agenda is divided into the four "W's." They are:

Welcome

Worship

Word

Works

The evangelism arm of the cell is categorized as **Works** in the meetings.

Make mention of your unbeliever friends in your cell meetings. Encourage all the cell members to pray for them daily. God will answer these prayers. The "Share the Vision" time is a critical part of every cell meeting. It is the time when all the members focus their attention on the fact that our primary task is reaching others. This is why cells multiply—every member is an evangelist!

A. BRIDGES TO UNBELIEVERS

A *SHARE GROUP* touches the lives of people who are a part of the *oikoses* of cell members. It focuses on a relationship already established, and the agenda is built from the many interests of those composing the group.

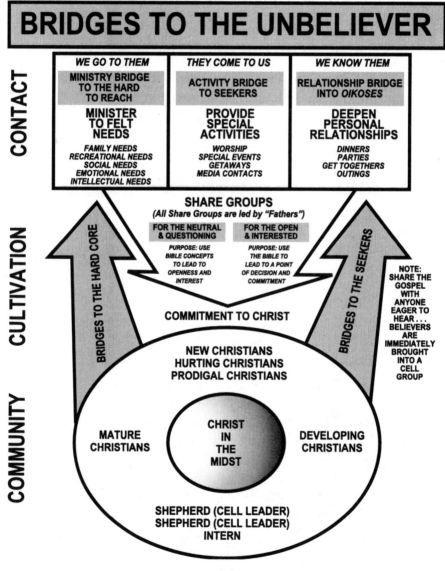

An *INTEREST GROUP* touches the lives of people who are not previously known to cell members. It focuses on a common interest shared by unbelievers. Interest Groups are to be considered by your Cell Group when you have third and fourth generation cell members prepared to go to a new geographical area and plant a cell from scratch.

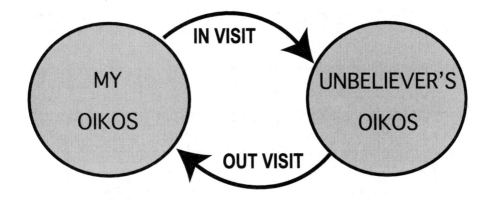

TWO TYPES OF VISITS:

"IN VISITS"

An "in visit" takes the believer *into* the household of an unbeliever. Parents, wives, husbands and friends are met. It is important to be visible to the people who surround your unsaved friends.

"OUT VISITS"

An "out visit" takes place when you invite the unbeliever *out* of his or her *oikos,* to visit in your *oikos.* Your Christian friends and cell members are the potential family of the unbeliever or new believer.

The book, *Building Bridges, Opening Hearts* is a valuable equipping tool to help you prepare your cell members to learn more about bridge building.

Building bridges to unbelievers takes time. If they spend some of their time in your world, and you spend some of your time in their world, a bridge will be built. Eventually, that bridge will allow the unbeliever to cross over to Christ. It will be meaningful if you devote a *Share The Vision* time to the discussion of "In" and "Out" Visits.

D. Tools to Share the Gospel With Unbelievers

1. Encouragement by the Holy Spirit

Effectively ministering to the unconverted connects you directly to the work of the Holy Spirit. In these Scriptures, note the clear link between the work of the Holy Spirit and the ministry of evangelism:

2. Witnessing Was Done When the Holy Spirit Came

"But you will receive power when the Holy Spirit comes on you; and you will be my witnesses in Jerusalem, and in all Judea and Samaria, and to the ends of the earth" (Acts 1:8).

3. Bold Sharing Was Done Through the Holy Spirit's Filling

"After they prayed, the place where they were meeting was shaken. And they were all filled with the Holy Spirit and spoke the word of God boldly" (Acts 4:31).

4. Conversions Resulted from the Encouragement of the Holy Spirit

"Then the church throughout Judea, Galilee and Samaria enjoyed a time of peace. It was strengthened; and encouraged by the Holy Spirit, it grew in numbers, living in the fear of the Lord" (Acts 9:31).

Often observing the presence of the Holy Spirit in a Christian opens Type "B" unbelievers to the gospel of Jesus Christ. When they witness His power, they have many questions that only the Gospel can answer. A Biblical explanation can then be added to the evidence of Christ's power.

5. Begin With Your Own Testimony

    a. Share your life before you became a Christian.
    b. Share the way you realized your need.
       (NOTE: since this is exactly the condition of your friend at this moment, be aware that this is an important point!)
    c. Explain how you went about receiving Christ into your life.
    d. Share what your life has been like since you made this commitment to Him.

6. Probe with An Appropriate Question

Here are some suggestions:

- "In your opinion, what is the greatest spiritual need in the world today?"
- "Have you been giving much thought to spiritual matters lately?"

7. Respond to the Answer With sensitivity

When the Holy Spirit is working in a person's life, you don't have to get "pushy." If the individual is obviously unwilling to continue with the discussion, change the subject and continue to pray. However, if there is a positive response, you must decide which direction to take: does this person need to be shown the John 3:16 diagram?

Expect the "encouragement of the Holy Spirit" to flow through you to those you are working with. Take advantage of every opportunity to show His powerful presence to unbelievers.

Once you have shared the diagram, ask the following question:

"I'd like to ask you: have you ever come to a point in your life where you allowed Jesus Christ to come into your heart, to live inside of you? Is there any reason why you would not want to choose that way today?"

(You pray, asking God to hear the prayer of your friend. Then let the person pray. Thank the Lord for coming into the life of your friend as a response to his/her prayer.)

8. Pray for Unbelievers

Finally on the basis of redemption—Christ's redemption, which purchased all mankind—we may say that each person is actually God's purchased possession, although he is still held by the Enemy. We must, through the prayer of faith, claim and take for God in the name of the Lord Jesus that which is rightfully His. This can be done only on the basis of redemption. This is not meant to imply that, because all persons have been purchased by God through redemption, they are automatically saved. They must believe and accept the gospel for themselves; our intercession enables them to do this.

To pray in the name of the Lord Jesus is to ask for, or to claim, the things which the blood of Christ has secured. Therefore, each individual for whom prayer is made should be claimed by name as God's purchased possession, in the name of the Lord Jesus and on the basis of His shed blood.

9. When you are praying for someone's salvation, include the following areas in your prayer:

   a. Present the person by name to Jesus Christ as His purchased possession.
   b. Pray against the powers of darkness that claim a hold on this person's life so that this person will have the freedom to choose to accept or reject Jesus Christ free from satan's interference or bondage.
   c. Pray that the Holy Spirit will draw this person toward Christ, convict him/her of their sin, and reveal the truth of God's plan for salvation.
   d. Pray that God will bring circumstances, people, and events into this person's life in order to reveal their need for Christ.

e. Pray that God will use you as an instrument to bring this person to Christ. Pray that the Holy Spirit will guide your every word and deed so that you will say and do the right thing at the right time. Pray that the light and joy of Christ will shine through your life as a testimony of the Christian faith.

As a cell leader, it is your commission to multiply your cell within approximately six months by adding from five to eight new believers to your group. What is the secret of the way cells do this in every part of the world? It is revealed in the following scriptures:

Live such good lives among the pagans that, though they accuse you of doing wrong, they may see your good deeds and glorify God on the day he visits us. (1 Peter 2:12)

And let us consider how we may spur one another on toward love and good deeds. (Hebrews 10:24)

In the same way, let your light shine before men, that they may see your good deeds and praise your Father in heaven. (Matthew 5:16)

In the same way, good deeds are obvious, and even those that are not cannot be hidden. (1 Timothy 5:25)

. . . but with good deeds, appropriate for women who profess to worship God. (1 Timothy 2:10)

. . . and is well known for her good deeds, such as bringing up children, showing hospitality, washing the feet of the saints, helping those in trouble and devoting herself to all kinds of good deeds. (1 Timothy 5:10)

Command them to do good, to be rich in good deeds, and to be generous and willing to share. (1 Timothy 6:18)

The *Share the Vision* slot should focus on how to increase the "good deeds" of the cell group. Sharing the gospel with others through relationships and "good deeds" caused the New Testament church to grow from 3,000 to 10,000 in a matter of weeks! Never forget that every one of us is a minister, and every cell group should engage every Christian member in serving the needs of unbelievers.

E. PROCEDURES FOR CONDUCTING "SHARE THE VISION" TIMES

Unbelievers In Our Oikoses		
Cell Member	*Type "A" Unbelievers*	*Type "B" Unbelievers*
John Smith	Elaine Smith Billy Kozak	Randall Evans Steven Logan Harvey Ligoner
Mary Smith	Evelyn Smith Dean Stevens	Lois Brown Linda Gopher
George Brown	Billy Brown Jim Stacker	Ellen Zimmerman William Zinnerman Carl Clower
Susan Slide		Matthew Garmon
Mickey Fall	James Cheshinre	Eddie Sterns Victor Tan
Harold Leaf	Abraham Simonson	Dwight Enginer Frank Fowler
Jean Leaf	Judy Libertana Robert Ruach	Elaine Turner Edward Turner
Happy Jones	Simon Tobler	Bill Bellington Nathan Quick

During the very first meeting of the cell group, the cell leader should ask each member to submit a list of all "Type A" and "Type B" unbelievers in their *oikoses*. The cell leader should then prepare a large poster card like the one in the above illustration. Each time the cell meets, this poster should be displayed at the beginning of the *Share The Vision* time. Prayer and discussion of the spiritual needs of these persons should be a part of every meeting.

Set your heart on the vision of seeing four to seven unbelievers coming into your cell group during each cycle. (Someone has said, "I'd rather shoot at a goal and *miss* it than shoot at *nothing* and *hit* it!") Be aware that all of the fast-growing cell churches around the world have cells that are able to achieve this goal. Satan will constantly tell you that is not possible. At the same time, Jesus is saying to you,

> *Do you not say, `Four months more and then the harvest'? I tell you, open your eyes and look at the fields! They are ripe for harvest. Even now the reaper draws his wages, even now he harvests the crop for eternal life, so that the sower and the reaper may be glad together. Thus the saying `One sows and another reaps' is true. I sent you to reap what you have not worked for. Others have done the hard work, and you have reaped the benefits of their labor."* (John 4:35-38)

Remind yourself constantly that the Holy Spirit is working within the *oikoses* that are connected to your cell group. The instructions of Jesus to the seventy in Luke 10 were very simple. First, they were to enter an *oikos*. Next, they were to offer their peace to *each person* in the *oikos*, knowing that a certain percentage of all people are restless within their spirits and are looking for answers to life's problems. Finally, once that person had been located and Jesus (who is our Peace!) had come to reside in that life, they were ordered to stay on, eating and drinking whatever was set before them.

It is crucial that your own value system is reshaped until your concern about spending time in the *oikoses* of people you know causes you to "eat and drink" with them! Do you hear Satan whispering to you, "That's ridiculous! You will have your hands full with the members of a cell group; there simply is not time to spend with unbelievers!" The "father of all lies" will seek to destroy your passion for lost souls, for he knows that a self-seeking cell group is no threat to the prisoners he controls.

WEEK 7
LEADERSHIP IN THE CELL

CHAPTER CONTENTS

A. Self-Analysis: Key Elements in Spiritual Leadership

B. Self-Analysis: Four Characteristics of a Spiritual Leader

C. The Jethro Principle

D. Jethro's Leadership Suggestions

E. Identifying Leaders

F. Three Types of Leadership

G. Involving Others in Ministry

H. How to Multiply Your Ministry

I. Practical Steps for Identifying and Equipping Interns

J. Basic Guidelines for Delegation

K. Four Kinds of Safe Places That Restore Spiritual Passion

OBJECTIVES

1. Self-evaluation of spiritual leadership characteristics.
2. Self-evaluation of the four characteristics of a spiritual leader.
3. Study Jethro's principles for selecting leaders.
4. Apply the leadership suggestions of Jethro to leading a cell.
5. Discern how to identify leaders in the cell group.
6. Evaluate three types of leadership to be found in the cell group.
7. Discover how to involve cell members in ministry.
8. Create a lifestyle to multiply the ministry of a cell leader.
9. Apply steps to identify and equip potential interns.
10. Study four kinds of ways burnout can be avoided.
11. Study basic guidelines to be used in delegating.

A. Self-Analysis: Key Elements in Spiritual Leadership

In this section, rate yourself by circling a 1, 2, or 3 in each place to show where you think your heart is:
1 = Heart for God Alone
2 = Divided Heart   *Example:*
3 = Heart for Self

There are eight key elements necessary for effective spiritual leadership:

1. A Heart for God
   [1|2|3] a. Obedience to God
   - Live your life according to the Word of God.
   - Live your life by conviction and not by circumstances or convenience.
   [1|2|3] b. Dependence upon God
   - "We live by faith, not by sight" (2 Corinthians 5:7)
   - "And without faith it is impossible to please God" (Hebrews 11:6)
   - Develop confidence in God in spite of circumstances and consequences.

2. A Heart for People
   [1|2|3] a. God places a high priority on people, and so do I. (1 Chronicles 14:2; Philippians 2:20-21)
   b. Check your attitudes towards people:
   [1|2|3] • Other people's failures challenge rather than annoy me.
   [1|2|3] • I serve people instead of using them.
   [1|2|3] • I seek to develop people rather than using them.
   [1|2|3] • I encourage people rather than criticizing them.
   [1|2|3] • I seek out problem people rather than avoiding them.
   [1|2|3] c. • I love and have a heart for people (Ephesians 4:2)

3. Committed to God's Word
   [1|2|3] a. Committed to knowing God's Word, I diligent study it. (2 Timothy 2:15)
   [1|2|3] b. I am committed to applying God's Word (James 1:22)

4. Demonstrates Discipline and Growth
    a. I show discipline . . .
[1|2|3] • In the use of my finances.
[1|2|3] • In practicing basic Christian principles.
    b. I am growing in . . .
[1|2|3] • Personal time with God.
[1|2|3] • Bible study times.
[1|2|3] • Time spent in the "Listening Room."

5. Pace-setter
[1|2|3] a. I lead by example, demonstrating what I want others to do.
[1|2|3] b. My philosophy is that more is *caught* than *taught.*

6. I Seek to Lead by Serving
[1|2|3] a. I desire to be a model of Christ (Mark 10:14; John 13:15)
[1|2|3] b. People are drawn first to my servanthood, rather than to my leadership.
[1|2|3] c. My service is an outward indication of my love for people.

7. **F. A. S. T**. Characteristics
    These are four characteristics of a strong leader. Check the boxes in the left margin if you feel these elements are true of you:
☐ a. **F**aithfulness: in little things (Matthew 25:21)
    • What is one thing you avoid doing because you think it is insignificant? _____
☐ b. **A**vailability: God is more concerned about my availability than my ability.
    • I am willing to do hard tasks.
    • I am willing to do humble tasks.
☐ c. **S**ubmissiveness: (Hebrews 13:17)
    • I am submitted to God's ordained leaders.
    • I submit not only when I agree with them, but all the time.
☐ d. **T**eachability: (Proverbs 9:8-9)
    • I seek to be a wise man rather than a cynic.
    • I can handle criticism or instructions from others.

94

8. I have a Vision—to multiply my cell.
[1|2|3] a. I allow God to stretch my vision.
[1|2|3] b. I have a vision for each cell member's development.
[1|2|3] c. I have asked God to show me His vision?

B. Self-Analysis: Four Characteristics of a Spiritual Leader

[1|2|3] 1. I seek to be a MODEL for the cell members.
[1|2|3] 2. I seek to MINISTER to people's needs with a servant's heart.
[1|2|3] 3. I seek to MOTIVATE people into action.
[1|2|3] 4. I seek to MAKE ministry happen.

C. The Jethro Principle

There are four qualities stated in this passage for someone who has oversight. They are:

1. "Capable men" . . . . .Ability
2. "Men who fear God" . . . . .Spirituality
3. "Trustworthy men" . . . . .Relationships
4. "Men who hate dishonest gain" . . .Ethics

D. Jethro's Leadership Suggestions

Check the boxes in the left margin if you feel these elements are true of you:

Jethro gave seven suggestions for those in leadership:

☐ 1. Shares the burden (Exodus 18:17-18, 23)
  • The leader will be able to stand the strain
  • The people will go home satisfied

☐ 2. Listens to good counsel (Exodus 18:19a)

☐ 3. Represents the people before God (Exodus 18:19b)

☐ 4. Teaches the people (Exodus 18:20a, 24)
  • Instruct them in the decrees, statutes and laws

☐ 5. Shows the people (Exodus 18:20b)
  • Model the way to live
  • Model the duties they are to perform

☐ 6. Selects leaders from amongst the people (Exodus 18:21)
  • Appoint them over specific units
  • Let them do assigned tasks
  • Be available for difficult problems

☐ 7. Implements the plan (Exodus 18:25)

E. Identifying Leaders

If you are a cell leader or an intern you are a shepherd. You are to care for the members of your cell. However, don't make the mistake of thinking that you are *the minister* of the cell. Every member is a minister! You are the *servant* of the ministers as you shepherd them.

What words are missing from Ephesians 4:16?

"From him (Christ) the whole body, joined and held together by every supporting ligament, grows and builds itself up in love, as _____ _____ does its work."

The words are *"each part."* The verse does not say that Christ's body grows as the *pastor* or the *cell leaders* do their work. The body grows as *each part* does its work.

This is important for you to remember. Your cell group will experience life and growth because you involve each member in ministry.

Your most crucial task is to raise up cell leaders from within your group. Every time a cell grows from seven or eight to fifteen, there will have to be two new Cell Leader Interns present at multiplication time.

GOD'S STANDARDS FOR LEADERS (1 SAMUEL 16:6-12)

What should we look for in leaders? Begin where God begins, with the heart! Out of what fills the heart, the mouth speaks and the feet walk. If a man has the right heart, God will, over a period of time, take care of things like maturity, zeal, knowledge and experience.

Look for a person with God's "**H. I. G. H.**" heart standards:

Holiness: a holy heart
   Is there sensitivity to sin and a heart of repentance?
Integrity: a heart of integrity
   Has the person proven to be trustworthy and honest, even in the small things?
Gratitude: a heart of gratitude
   Does murmuring and complaining fill his mouth?
Humility: a heart of humility
   Does he or she come as a master, or as a servant?

Dion Robert now has 80,000 cell members in Abidjan, Ivory Coast, Africa. He multiplies his cells every four to five months, and usually produces *three Cell Leader Interns* in each multiplication! After 20 years, he and his people have learned how to develop new believers rapidly and develop them to lead cells.

It is important to note that Pastor Dion explains it takes about two years before a new convert is ready to serve as a cell leader intern. We recognize that after 20 years he has a backlog of trained people. If a cell church is in its first, second, or third generation, it will take longer. Nevertheless, this should be your pattern of equipping:

There are seven stages to his equipping cycle:

Active participation in the work of God → New Birth • Integrated into a family • Orientation towards a new life style • Development of life in the Spirit • Discovery of gifts and ministry • Training for the service of God

1   2   3   4   5   6   7

THE EQUIPPING CYCLE

Each new Christian is carefully guided by the Cell Leader and the Intern. Each one is evaluated, guided, and developed to leave behind old values and begin to live by Kingdom values. More and more ministry tasks are assigned. Each of these stations in the journey are carefully monitored and ministry tasks are slowly assigned.

From the entry of a cell member into your group, you should carefully assess the growth pattern which will lead you to select potential cell leader interns. Here is a list of questions you should ask about your cell members:

EXPERIENCE   Does the potential leader have a personal experience with the Lord from which he or she is growing in grace and love?

EXALTATION   Does the potential leader exalt God out of a joyous and positive heart or is he or she a complainer with a negative attitude?

EQUIPPING   Does the potential leader have a servant's heart and the gifts necessary to equip others in the tasks he or she has already completed?

EDIFICATION   Does the potential leader contribute to the building up of the Body of Christ at both the cell and congregational level?

EVANGELISM   Does the potential leader contact the lost, form relationships with them and lead them to commitment within the context of a cell community?

EXAMPLE   Does the potential leader model the life of Christ in action and attitude at home, at work and in the world?

F. Three Types of Leadership

According to Michael E. Gerber in his book, The "E-Myth," there are three types of leadership. We all have an *Entrepreneur, Manager, and Technician* inside us. If they were equally balanced, we would be describing an incredibly competent individual. But the three are seldom balanced in one person. Therefore, we must depend upon each other to provide these three important leadership functions.

ENTREPRENEUR	MANAGER	TECHNICIAN
VISIONARY *DREAMER* FUTURE	PRAGMATIST *PLANNER* PAST	DOER *FIXER* PRESENT
MOTTO "If you want it done right, create a new . . ."	**MOTTO** "if you want it done right, train a good worker"	**MOTTO** "If you want it done right, do it yourself"
BOUNDARY HOW MANY MANAGERS CAN BE IN HIS VISION? • Builds a house and plans the next one • Sees opportunities • What wall should the ladder be against? • Needs change	**BOUNDARY** HOW MANY TECHNICIANS CAN HE SUPERVISE? • Builds a house and lives in it forever • Sees problems • How do I best get the ladder to the wall? • Craves order	**BOUNDARY** HOW MUCH CAN HE DO BY HIMSELF? • Never stops building the house • Sees a job to do • How many times do I go up and down? • Wants activity
WORLDVIEW *OPPORTUNITIES ABOUND EVERYWHERE* • Creates Things To Be Put In Rows	**WORLDVIEW** *MESSES MUST BE CLEANED UP* • Puts Things Into Neat Rows	**WORLDVIEW** *PRODUCES BREAD TO EAT AT TONIGHT'S DINNER* • Fixes The Things That Are In Neat Rows

G. Involving Others in Ministry

It is your jobs as a shepherd to model friendship, caring concern and ministry to the rest of the group and then to involve them in ministry themselves. Here are several ways you can do that:

1. Recognize God at work.

God is working through each person, young and old, in your cell group. Each has beautiful gifts and abilities that God has given them to bless and touch others. One of them may be very good at encouraging others, another may have a gift of intercession, while still another is good at organizing events. There is a great diversity in the ways God anoints people for service.

However, because of Satan's deception and individuals' negative past experiences, people are often unable to see the ways God is using them. Your job as a cell leader is to encourage and affirm people by telling them how you see God using them. Have you been touched by God through a cell member this week? Let this person know about it.

2. Involve people in ministry tasks.

As you see God using people, involve them in various ministry tasks. If they are good organizationally, ask them to help plan the next social event of your cell. If they have a ministry of encouragement, involve them in visiting or calling members in need. Also, give members responsibilities relating to your cell meetings—things like leading the icebreaker, guiding the ministry time, sharing their testimony, helping with the children's time and hosting the meeting.

3. Involve members in ministry roles.

When members have proven to be reliable in ministry tasks, involve them in special tasks. Delegate an entire portion of the cell ministry to these persons. For example, if someone has a heart for worship and some musical ability, you can ask this person to serve the cell group as the worship leader. Someone with a special concern for children could be assigned to organize weekly ministry to the children. Someone else might be asked to keep a prayer journal for the cell, while another member might be asked to phone those who missed the cell meeting, getting their prayer concerns and letting them know of upcoming events.

A very important ministry is performed by the cell leader intern. A group cannot have too many interns. Because this role is so important to the future of the group, you need to identify and recruit new cell leader interns, even as you yourself are serving as one.

H. How to Multiply Your Ministry

The only one way for you to multiply and extend your ministry is for you to recruit interns. If you do not raise up interns under you, your ministry will eventually end.

By raising up interns, you will see you ministry multiplied many times over. The Apostle Paul gives us an example of internship. He was a church planting intern under Barnabas. He then interned many others, including Silas and Titus. He gave Timothy this charge:

> *"And the things you have heard me say in the presence of many witnesses entrust to reliable men who will also be qualified to teach others." (2 Timothy 2:2)*

Notice that what Timothy learned from Paul was to be passed on to others, who would train still another generation of leaders. You can see the widening circles of influence:

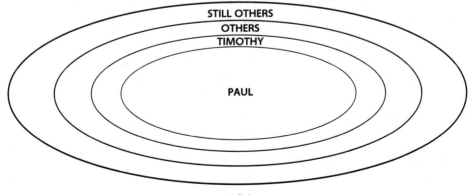

I. Practical Steps for Identifying and Equipping Interns.

1. Pray.

Jesus explained the first step in recruiting leaders is prayer:

> When he (Jesus) saw the crowds, he had compassion on them, because they were harassed and helpless, like sheep without a shepherd. Then he said to his disciples, "The harvest is plentiful but the workers are few. Ask the Lord of the harvest, therefore, to send out workers into his harvest field." (Matthew 9:36-38)

Jesus did not say to pray for a harvest. There is already an abundant harvest. What we need is more shepherds, more workers. The way to get them is through prayer. Besides mobilizing unseen dynamics, prayer also enables us to hear God's voice and to cooperate with Him in leadership development. As a cell intern, this is the time for you to begin praying for God to raise up more leaders under your ministry.

Do not be praying for just *one* intern; pray for *several* each cell cycle. This is important because, as you'll discover, interns progress at different rates and some take more than one cell cycle before they are ready to become cell leaders themselves.

2. Give responsibilities to potential interns.

Some of the persons who will make the best future leaders are not the ones you would select at first. One of the best ways to discover those with the most potential is give them specific tasks and responsibilities before you approach them about being an intern.

Invite potential interns to go with you when you visit cell members. Ask them to lead the edification time or prayer time in the cell meeting. As you involve people in different ministry tasks, watch them closely. Do they have a heart for others? Do they follow instructions well? Are they persons of prayer? You are basically looking for individuals who have a heart for God, a heart for others and an attitude of cooperation.

By involving persons in ministry you also build their confidence, making it easier for them to say "yes" when they are asked to become an intern.

3. Consult with your Zone Supervisor.

When you are a cell leader it is important for you to consult with your zone supervisor before asking someone to serve as an intern. Your supervisor may know of problems in someone's life that you are not aware of. Likewise, they may also see potential in someone you might overlook. You are much more likely to make a wise decision if you are praying and thinking together with your supervisor.

Another reason that you must talk to your zone supervisor is because you want the recruitment of interns to be a joint decision. If an intern doesn't work out, you can't be blamed personally if you made the decision with your supervisor.

4. Recruit.

Recruiting is an important step. Take the time to meet personally with a person before you ask them to be a cell leader intern. Affirm the potential that you see and the ways that you have seen God working. If the person is not ready to say "yes" immediately, suggest you both pray about the matter and talk again after a few days. Let the person know that there will be special training offered by the church to fully equip for the cell leader ministry.

5. Pray and plan together weekly.

When you become a cell leader, meet your interns at a convenient time so that you can together pray for your cell members and plan your cell meetings and other activities. When you meet, take time to invite God to work in each of your cell member's lives and ask God to unite them in fellowship, ministry and outreach. Take time to plan to make phone calls, contacting special persons, and making preparation for your cell meetings. Remember to regularly schedule times for the cell group to entertain unbelievers with special events.

6. Give away your ministry.

Increasingly give away your ministry to your intern or interns. At the beginning of the cell cycle you will probably be carrying about 80% of the leadership. At the end of the cell cycle you should only carry about 20%. It should look something like this:

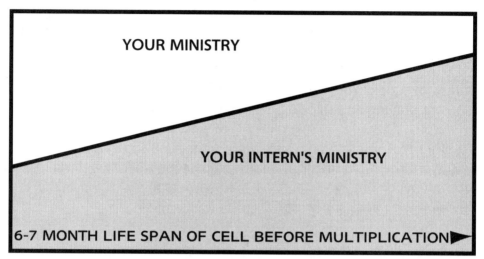

YOUR MINISTRY

YOUR INTERN'S MINISTRY

6-7 MONTH LIFE SPAN OF CELL BEFORE MULTIPLICATION▶

The last few months you should do very little. Not only does this give you a rest time during each cycle but it also enables your intern(s) to develop confidence in their abilities. This also allows the cell members to develop confidence in your intern's ability, making the way for a successful multiplication of your cell. When raising up interns, remember John the Baptist's words: *"He must become greater; I must become less" (John 3:30).*

7. Encourage profusely.

Interns need correction, but even more they need encouragement. Use the "8:2 Principle": find eight things to praise for every two things you choose to correct. It is your job to build your intern's confidence and faith. If an intern could have better handled a situation, begin by asking for any thoughts the person might have about other ways the situation could have been handled. By starting this way, you will see how situations are perceived. You can then add your own thoughts to the ideas and together work out better solutions to problem cases.

8. The Value of Interns

It is initially more work to recruit an intern. You need to involve them in ministry and planning, taking time to equip and encourage them. However, this extra work pays off almost immediately because the effectiveness of your cell group increases tremendously. You will soon feel your own load becoming lighter and lighter.

The short term benefits are far outweighed by the long terms ones. By identifying and training future leaders you will multiply your influence many times over, extending Christ's caring ministry and power into the future and around the world.

J. Basic Guidelines for Delegation

1. Delegation does not remove the leader from responsibility. A certain responsibility always rests on the delegator. The leader must do follow up, checking on the needs and progress of the one who was given responsibility.

2. Delegate everything you can. Do only what cannot be delegated. Don't do something that someone else can do. There are plenty of jobs that others cannot or will not do.

3. Perhaps one of the reasons leaders fail to delegate is simply that they are not sure how they should go about it. The following nine guidelines will be helpful to you. Read this list frequently as you develop your ministry as a cell leader:

4. Nine Guidelines for Delegation

   a. The leader should *recognize his own limits*. He must remember that other parts of the body can function better in some areas. Discover the capabilities in the lives of the other members of your cell group and let them share your load.

   b. The leader should *determine what needs to be delegated*. He needs to note what jobs he must be free from in order to perform best in his primary responsibilities.

c. The leader should *determine why the task is to be delegated.* Some jobs will be delegated to give him more time; others will be delegated to sharpen the skills of another person. Still others may be delegated to show recognition.

d. The leader should *match the person with the delegated task.*
   • Who would be best suited to this task?
   • What gifts are involved?
   • Who has shown interest in this area of service?
   • Who will have the time to devote to it?

e. The leader should *exhibit confidence in the person selected.* How the task is assigned is important. Does the leader express both confidence and high expectation, or does he communicate the idea that "you are my last hope, since I couldn't get anyone else"?

f. The leader should *define clearly his expectations.* Unclear objectives are deadly and ensure failure. Here is where a job description is needed so that everyone views the job in a similar way.

g. The leader should *clearly define the boundaries of authority.* A great deal of frustration or animosity can develop if there is not agreement on what the person can or cannot do.

h. The leader should *provide the needed resources for the task.* The resources may include money, necessary information, training or access to certain people or equipment.

i. The leader should *do follow up.* Regular meetings or some system for adequate feedback must be set up.

5. Questions About Delegation

   How well do you delegate responsibility? As you look at these questions, ask yourself if you are satisfied or dissatisfied with what you have done.

   • Have I been successful in retaining my cell members?
   • Am I exploring and discovering the gifts and talents of my cell members?

- Are cell members demonstrating spiritual and professional growth under my leadership?
- Do I take time daily to relax and think creatively?
- Am I able to leave my leadership role for periods of time with the assurance that the work will be done well?
- Am I discovering new leaders in the cell group?
- Do those I have equipped sponsor others effectively?

K. Four Kinds of Safe Places That Restore Spiritual Passion

(Adapted from "Restoring Your Spiritual Passion" by Gordon MacDonald)

In 2 Timothy 4:16 Paul wrote to his intern:

"Watch your life and doctrine closely. Persevere in them, because if you do you will save both yourself and your hearers."

As a shepherd, it is important that you watch out for your own spiritual life at the same time you are watching over the members of your cell group. Do not fail to monitor your own spiritual life as you watch that of others. In Psalm 63 we are told of several special places where we can nurture our relationship with God:

1. The Sanctuary

   "So I have looked upon thee in the sanctuary, beholding Thy power and glory. Because Thy steadfast love is better than life, my lips will praise thee." (Psalm 63:2-3, RSV)

   "When I tried to understand all this, it was oppressive to me till I entered the sanctuary of God; then I understood their final destiny." (Psalm 73:16,17)

   The weariness that comes from intimidation or defeat, the fatigue that comes from being drained by people who attempt to dominate our world, and the exhaustion that comes from fighting spiritual battles need to be viewed in the context of an almighty God. And that is exactly what David did in his safe place. It became a sanctuary for eternal perspectives.

2. The Night Room

As David pondered his outer world in the desert, a second kind of safe place came to mind. There he had met God in the past. It was his place of rest, where he usually slept, the night room in his palace.

"On my bed I remember You; I think of You through the watches of the night. Because You are my help, I sing in the shadow of Your wings." (Psalm 63:6-7)

3. The Protective Wings

"In a desert land he found him, in a barren and howling waste. He shielded him and cared for him; he guarded him as the apple of his eye, like an eagle that stirs up its nest and hovers over its young, that spreads its wings to catch them and carries them on its pinions." (Deuteronomy 32:10-11)

"He will cover you with his feathers, and under his wings you will find refuge; his faithfulness will be your shield and rampart." (Psalm 91:4)

"Have mercy on me, O God, have mercy on me, for in you my soul takes refuge. I will take refuge in the shadow of your wings until the disaster has passed." (Psalm 57:1)

4. The Strong Hands

Confidence is a state of mind and heart that permits a person to act with assurance that yesterday's defeat or failure will turn into tomorrow's victory. It is a sense of a new source of power from beyond ourselves—a power that is available in unlimited amounts to us as Christians.

"I stay close to you; your right hand upholds me." (Psalm 63:8)

The grasp of the Father's hand was a safe place for David. Like a frightened child devoid of any confidence, his soul reached out to the outstretched hand of God.

It is in these safe places that we hear God's secrets whispered to our inner spirit. Where are your safe places? Where is it that God can meet you and share His secrets?

WEEK 8
PRAYER IN THE CELL

CHAPTER CONTENTS

A. How to Pray for the Lost

B. Prayerwalking

C. Journaling

D. Praying for Leaders

OBJECTIVES

1. Learn to pray for unsaved relatives and friends by breaking strongholds.

2. Know the value of prayerwalking.

3. Learn to integrate prayerwalking into daily lifestyle.

4. Know the different types of prayerwalks.

5. Learn to use journaling as a means to discern God's voice.

6. Know the importance of intercession for leaders.

A. How to Pray for the Lost

Believers everywhere are burdened for the unsaved or backslidden loved ones, however, many are praying in a spirit of fear and worry instead of faith.

We need light on how to pray, we need direction on what to pray and a promise or word from God on which to base our faith. Praise God—He never fails to give such needed help.

Perhaps because the salvation of some seems to be an impossibility, we need to know the Scripture in Mark 10:27, "*All things are possible with God.*" Also, the following scripture should often be quoted from memory:

> "*The weapons we fight with are not the weapons of the world. On the contrary, they have divine power to demolish strongholds. We demolish arguments and every pretension that sets itself up against the knowledge of God, and we take captive every thought to make it obedient to Christ.*"
> (*2 Corinthians 10:4,5*)

These verses show the mighty power of our spiritual weapons. We must pray that all of this will be accomplished in the people for whom we're concerned. Know that the works of the enemy will be torn down.

The basis of redemption is the solid foundation for our prayers. In reality, Christ's redemption purchased all mankind. We may say that each person is actually God's purchased possession, although he is still held by the enemy. We must through the prayer of faith, claim and take for God in the name of the Lord Jesus that which is rightfully His. This can be done only on the basis of redemption.

This is not meant to imply that, because all persons have been purchased by God through redemption, they are automatically saved. They must believe and accept the Gospel for themselves. Our intercession enables them to do this.

To pray in the name of the Lord Jesus is to ask for, or to claim, the things which the blood of Christ has secured. Each individual for whom prayer is made should be claimed by name as God's purchased possession, in the name of the Lord Jesus and on the basis of His shed blood.

We tear down all the works of satan, such as false doctrine, unbelief, atheistic teaching, and hatred, which the enemy may have built into their thinking. We must pray that their very thoughts will be brought into captivity to the obedience of Christ.

With the authority of the name of the Lord Jesus, we must claim their deliverance from the power and persuasion of the evil one, the lord of this world. We should also pray that their conscience may be convicted, that God may bring them to the point of repentance, and that they may listen and believe as they hear or read the Word of God. Our prayer must be that God's will and purposes may be accomplished in and through them.

Intercession must be persistent—not to persuade God, but because of the enemy. Our prayers and resistance are against the enemy—the powers and rulers of darkness. It is our duty, before God, to fight for the souls whom Christ died for. For just as some must preach to them the good news of redemption, others must fight the powers of darkness on their behalf through prayer.

Satan yields only what and when he must, and he renews his attacks in subtle ways. Therefore, prayer must be definite and persistent, even long after definite results are seen. We must pray for the new Christian even after he begins to be established in the faith.

We will find that as we pray, the Holy Spirit will give new directions. Thank God that spiritual weapons are mighty and that our authority in Christ is far above all the authority of the rulers, powers, and forces of darkness, so that the enemy must yield. It will take faith and patience and persistence.

Note that *"The Spirit gives life; the flesh counts for nothing"* (John 6:63) and that *"the letter kills, but the spirit gives life."* (2 Corinthians 3:6). Therefore, we must constantly seek the motivation of the Holy Spirit in our hearts, in our faith, in our prayers, and in our testimony. It is most important also that we confess our own sins and have them forgiven. The enemy will use every possible means to silence our intercession and to block our attack against him. We must not only understand the enemy, our authority in Christ, and how to use our spiritual weapons but also how to wear the armor that God has provided for our protection. The equipped and protected, need not have any fear. But let us always remember that we have no power and no authority other than that of Christ.

"But thanks be to God who always leads us in triumphal procession in Christ" (2 Corinthians 2:14). *"The one who is in you is greater than the one who is in the world"* (1 John 4:4).

When you are praying for someone's salvation, include the following areas in your prayer:

1. Present the person by name to Jesus Christ as His purchased possession.

2. Pray against the powers of darkness that claim a hold on this person's life so that this person will have the freedom to choose to accept or reject Jesus Christ apart from satan's interference or bondage.

3. Pray that the Holy Spirit will draw this person toward Christ, convict them of their sin, and reveal to them the truth of God's plan for salvation.

4. Pray that God will bring circumstances, people, and events into this person's life in order to reveal to them their need for Christ.

5. Pray that God will use you as an instrument to bring this person to Christ. Pray that the Holy Spirit will guide your every word and deed so that you will say and do the right thing at the right time. Pray that the light and joy of Christ will shine through your life as a testimony of the Christian faith.

6. Pray that Christ's life, character and nature will be formed in the person.

B. Prayerwalking
(Adapted from "Prayerwalking" by Graham Kendrick and John Houghton)

1. Prayerwalking is a Strategy for:

   a. Breaking free from a "straightjacket" prayer meeting.
      The general image of a prayer meeting is that of a dull routine gathering, usually lacking in vision and direction. Such meetings are attended by the minority of Church members. Those who attend them faithfully do not know how to get out of the rut, while those not attending will find no motivation to get in. Prayerwalking, on the other hand, breaks the mould of such static meetings.

   b. Moving the church into the community.
      Prayerwalking helps to get the church outside its buildings and into the community in spiritual and numerical strength. Although the primary aim is not evangelism, it gets people asking what you are doing. Sometimes, the passer-by may ask you to pray for him. God will guide you even as he did Philip in Acts 8:26-38.

   c. Making unexpected contacts with the lost.
      In prayerwalking, you get to meet new people. Occasionally these contacts can lead to conversion. Sometimes you may feel led to witness to a passer-by whom the Lord has laid on your heart. He may be saved, or healed, or both! Prayerwalking provides that crucial ingredient: being there!

   d. Increasing our awareness.
      Prayerwalking "earths" our heavenly intercessions. Many Christians pray for their neighborhood without actually encountering it. We do not know what's there because we do not do the legwork to find out. Through prayerwalking, Christians can discover roads they never knew existed, including local clubs and institutions they had previously ignored.

e. Enlarging our vision.
    It is easy for our vision to be limited by our present activities. Prayerwalking will open up new areas, and we will find ourselves praying for other churches, schools, prisons, etc., which we have overlooked in the past.

f. Invading satan's territory.
    Prayerwalking takes us bodily and spiritually into territories where satan has a vested interest.

g. Redeeming the time.
    Prayerwalking releases us from activities which rob us of our prayer time. In spite of the benefits of cars and modern appliances, we still complain of having no time to pray. The reason is simply because we are surrounded by "time robbers." The more sophisticated the culture around us, the more we become prisoners of time demands. The television set, the telephone, the newspaper and magazines are all examples of "time robbers" which steal frightening amounts of our time with all the subtlety of a pickpocket. You do not know the time is gone until you need it for something important, like prayer.

h. Penetrating our streets with righteousness.
    Getting righteous people out, praying on the streets as a regular part of life, is one of the most effective ways of freeing our towns from the scourge of robbery, rape and violence. Through such prayers, the church can change the balance of spiritual power, and make our streets safer places for people in the neighborhood.

i. Improving our fellowship
    A cell group, prayerwalking regularly, will draw closer to one another in spirit. Even those who do not know each other will find relationships forming over a short span of time. Prayerwalking is constructive work performed together. The team can enjoy the satisfaction of a job well done and look forward to the shared fruit of their labors.

2. How Does Prayerwalking Work?

Prayerwalking in essence is no more than the conscious combination of two of our most natural and basic human abilities: walking and talking.

It consist of three elements:
- Outside
- On the move
- Talking to God

a. Outside

Prayerwalking can be done anywhere, but it is recommended that you start with your immediate neighborhood. Weather conditions need not be a hindrance. It can be done anytime of the day or night that is suitable for you. Part of the beauty of prayerwalking is its sheer flexibility. There is no need to always schedule it. It can fit between other tasks.

b. On the move

Prayerwalking is not meant for hikers only. A short afternoon or evening stroll can become a powerful prayer time. Five minutes is better than nothing. It's not the distance you cover that matters, but the effectiveness of your prayer that counts. The pace does not need to be continuous. Frequent stops can be used to your advantage too! You may want to stop in front of an escort agency, etc., in order to pray against their influence.

c. Talking to God

The simplest strategy in prayerwalking is to go for a walk with one or two friends. Briefly discuss what you want to pray about and then begin to converse with the Lord. As with all conversations, it's okay to interchange between speakers and to interject your agreement while someone is praying. When one topic is covered, you can talk about the next thing on your hearts and repeat the process.

Quite often, the things you see while you walk will stimulate you to prayer. Sometimes the Lord will lay on your heart to pray for particular people who pass by you in the street. You can also have periods of silent prayer, times when you agree to walk alone, or occasions when you speak in tongues. It is also all right to worship the Lord and even sing, if that comes naturally.

3. Types of Prayerwalks

   a. During the normal business of life
      Prayer walking as a way of redeeming time can add spiritual significance to some of our activities. For example,
      • Walking to and from the bus-stops.
      • When we walk the dog.
      • When we are in the check-out line at the supermarket or in any waiting situation.
      • Prayerwalk to corridors of your block of houses.
      • Try to spend half an hour once a week prayerwalking the neighborhood and praying for every house.
      • When on holiday, pray with your companion as you walk around seeing the sights.
      • Take an evening stroll with your spouse or a friend instead of watching TV.

   b. Make Prayerwalking a planned cell activity
      Prayer walking is ideal for a cell. Almost any meeting can be adapted to include prayerwalking. Allocate the first half hour before the meeting for prayerwalking.

   c. Church-wide Walks
      Leaders can organize a church prayer invasion of an area. The aim is to mobilize every member on one evening or afternoon to pray for a neighborhood. Such united exercises can be done city-wide.

C. Journaling: a Means of Discerning God's Voice

Journaling is simply keeping a notebook of one's prophetic words, visions, dreams or prayers and what one senses to be the interpretations or answers. Journaling helps us discern the voice of God speaking to our hearts. We have 150 Psalms that were written this way, as well as the books of the Prophets and the book of Revelation. Clearly it is a common Biblical experience. In 1 Chronicles 28:12-19, we have an example of journaling that did not comprise part of Scripture, thus exemplifying the exact procedure we are recommending.

God is speaking to His children much of the time. However, we often cannot differentiate His voice from our own thoughts. Therefore, we are timid about stepping out in faith. If we have learned to clearly discern His voice speaking within us, we will be much more confident in our walk in the Spirit. Journaling is a way of sorting out God's thoughts from our thoughts.

One of the greatest benefits of using a journal during your communion with the Lord is that it allows you to receive freely the spontaneous flow of ideas that come to your mind. This is done in faith, believing that they are from Jesus, without short-circuiting them by subjecting them to rational and sensory doubt. You can write in your journal in faith, believing the thoughts are from the Lord, knowing that you will be able to test them later.

One person explains, "I found that before I began keeping a journal, I would ask God for an answer to a question, and as soon as an idea came into my mind, I would immediately question whether the idea was from God or from myself. In so doing, I was short-circuiting the intuitive flow of the Spirit by subjecting it to a rational doubt. I have found that the flow of God is arrested by doubt."

"I would get one idea from God and doubt that it was from Him, and therefore get no more. Now, by writing it down, I can receive whole pages by faith, knowing I will have ample time to test it later."

"And without faith it is impossible to please God"
(Hebrews 11:6a).

There are two words for "word" in the Greek. One of them is *"rhema,"* which refers to "the spoken words of God." The other is *"logos,"* which typically refers to "the written words of God." While too much should not be made of these distinctions, it is important to know that God speaks today. Keeping a journal greatly facilitates the flow of *"rhema"* into your heart. Maintaining a journal also keeps your mind occupied and on track as you receive God's words. Another advantage of writing revelation down is given in Habakkuk 2:2,3. Habakkuk was told that he should write down what he had received, because there would be a period of time before it came about. Therefore, your journal becomes an accurate reminder of unfulfilled revelations or prophetic words that God has given you.

A believer writes, "After keeping a journal for 6 years, I cannot fully express how it has deepened my relationship with Christ. It has been one of the most helpful tools I have discovered for growth in the spirit." Obviously, automatic writing is satan's counterpart to journaling. Those who have experienced automatic writing before becoming a Christian tell us that in automatic writing, a spirit comes and controls their hands, whereas in journaling there is a spontaneous flow of ideas birthed by God in their hearts. These ideas are then recorded by a person, who has his or her hand freely under his control.

1. Practical Suggestions for Journaling

   a. Since you are coming to meet with your Creator and Sustainer and to commune with Him, your time of journaling should be when you are in prime condition and are not overcome by fatigue or the cares of the world. Many find early morning to be the best time. Some find the middle of the night best for them. Find your best time and use it to be with Him.

   b. A simple spiral-bound notebook is sufficient, but you may choose to type your thoughts. One man even communes with God in his car using a tape recorder: he simply speaks forth the words he feels are coming from God.

   c. Keep your journal out of reach of others and use codes when necessary. As you bare your soul to God and He counsels you, some of your materials will be of a private nature and should be kept confidential. Grammar and spelling are not important when journaling.

d. Date all entries.

e. Include in your journal your communion with God, your dreams and their interpretations, visions and images the Lord gives you, and personal feelings and events that matter to you (that is, angers, fears, hurts, anxieties, disappointments, joys and thanksgiving).

f. As you begin journaling, you will find the Holy Spirit granting you healing, love and affirmation as He speaks edification, exhortation and comfort to your heart for others (1 Corinthians 14:3). He will lead you into a fuller love relationship with Jesus and provide the encouragement and self-acceptance the Father wants to grant to you.

Then, as time goes on, allow it to expand into a flow of the gifts of the Holy Spirit (that is, prophecy, words of wisdom, words of knowledge, discerning of spirits, etc., which are written in your journal).

If you seek to use your journal to cultivate the gift before you have sharpened your journaling ability through use, you may find that your mistakes will set you back so severely that it will be hard to press on with the use of a journal. After your journaling skill is firmly established through much use, you will find the gifts beginning to flow naturally through it. Allow them to come in their time.

g. Have a good knowledge of the Bible so that God can draw upon that knowledge as you journal. Not only is "*rhema*" tested against the "*logos*", but it is also built upon the *Logos,* the written word of God, the Bible. God told Joshua to meditate, confess and act upon the Law of God day and night so that God could give him success (Joshua 1:8). If I will yield my heart and mind and life to obey God's principles, and then pause in dependence upon Him in a given situation, He will lead and guide me through a flow of spontaneous thought.

h. Those wanting to add more structure to their journaling may use the first couple of pages to list people and items God burdens them to pray for regularly.

i. When you begin your journal, write down the question you have, rather than just thinking it. This simple act will assist greatly in discerning the Lord's response.

3. Safeguards for Your Journey Inward

a. Cultivate a humble, teachable spirit. Never develop the attitude: "God told me, and that's all there is to it." All revelation is to be tested. In learning any new skill, mistakes are inevitable. Accept them as part of the learning process, and go on.

b. Have a good knowledge of the Bible so that you can test the "rhema" against the "logos."

c. God gives special revelation in areas He has entrusted us with responsibility. A housewife will receive revelation for the home. A husband will receive revelation for shepherding the home and functioning in his business. As a cell leader, you will receive revelation for the cell over which God has made you responsible. Along with God-given authority comes God-given revelation to wisely exercise that authority. Therefore, look for revelation in the areas over which God has given you authority and responsibility. Stay away from an ego trip in which you begin seeking revelation for areas where God has not given you responsibility.

d. Be fully committed to the pastoral leadership; walk under the guidance of a spiritual counselor. Realize that until your journaling is submitted and confirmed, it should be regarded as "what you think God is saying."

e. Ascertain whether your journaling experience is leading you to greater wholeness and ability to love God and share about Him. If your experiences become destructive to you, you are in contact with the wrong spirits and you should seek out your spiritual counselor immediately.

f. PRAY—"God, may You teach me to discern clearly the flow of Your voice and Your vision within my heart."

4. Journaling: A Way to Organize Your Prayer Time

Here's a suggestion to get started in journaling:

Divide the notebook into four sections, called "P. A. R. T.:"

a. **P**raise—write personal praise prayers after reading four to five psalms.

b. **A**dmit—honestly discuss your temper, impatience and other shortcomings with the One who already knows them and loves you regardless.

c. **R**equests—"Morning by morning, O Lord, you hear my voice; morning by morning I lay my requests before you and wait in expectation." (Psalm 5:3). Each morning, bring your requests before God and wait for his reply.

d. **T**hanks—daily acknowledge that you recognize God's touch. His love, and His intimacy in your life.

Later in the day sit down and listen. Write down and organize any thoughts, prayers and ideas that God impresses upon your heart during your Bible reading time.

5. Areas of Prayer

As we examine the Lord's prayer and other prayers in the Bible, we find that there are various areas of prayer in which one can participate. The areas that are listed with the next section for you, will not all be found in every prayer session, nor will they follow a legalistic order or a rigid time slot. They are to flow as directed by the Holy Spirit. We are to always "pray in the Spirit" (Ephesians 6:18), meaning that our prayers are to be inspired, guided, energized, and sustained by the Holy Spirit.

As we pray, we should cultivate a constant openness to seeing and sensing the spiritual realm. Through dreams and visions, we are able to see with the eyes of faith those things which God is doing, as

Jesus did (John 5:19-21; 8:38). Through our sensing peace, burdens and other movings in our spirits, we are able to feel those things which God is feeling and impressing upon us. By so doing, our prayer life will transcend from dry rationalism into the beauty and power of spiritual experiences. For prayer to be meaningful, it must rise above simple rationalism.

a. Confession of sins

1 John 1:7-10: "But if we walk in the light, as he is in the light, we have fellowship with one another, and the blood of Jesus, his Son, purifies us from all sin. If we claim to be without sin, we deceive ourselves and the truth is not in us. If we confess our sins, he is faithful and just and will forgive us our sins and purify us from all unrighteousness. If we claim we have not sinned, we make him out to be a liar and his word has no place in our lives."

Our sins separate us from God, and He hides His presence from us (Isaiah 59:1,2). We must deal with all our sins every day, or prayer becomes a meaningless, spiritless, fruitless and agonizing endeavor, rather than a meaningful, spiritual, fruitful, and delightful encounter with God.

b. Praise, thanksgiving, singing, worship and adoration

Psalm 100:1-4: "Shout for joy to the Lord, all the earth. Serve the Lord with gladness; come before him with joyful songs. Know that Lord is God. It is he who made us, and we are his; we are his people, the sheep of his pasture. Enter his gates with thanksgiving and his courts with praise; give thanks to him and praise his name."

Having intimate communion early in your prayer time gets your mind off yourself and makes you God-conscious, which puts you into contact with God. Praise and thanksgiving may be used as the culmination of your petitions to express your faith in God's overcoming power.

c. Receiving: waiting, watching, listening, writing and meditating

Psalm 46:10a: "Be still and know that I am God"

Ecclesiastes 5:1,2: "Guard your steps when you go to the house of God. Go near to listen rather than to offer the sacrifice of fools, who do not know that they do wrong. Do not be quick with your mouth, do not be hasty in your heart to utter anything before God. God is in heaven and you are on earth, so let your words be few."

Once you have "settled down" (through Bible reading, praise, tongues, or any other means that is conducive to you) and are in communion with God in your spirit, you are to wait quietly before Him, looking to Him and recording those things He will say to you.

d. Personal Petitions

Matthew 6:11: "Give us today our daily bread."

Matthew 7:7: "Ask and it will be given to you; seek and you will find; knock and the door will be opened to you."

Psalm 50:15: "And call upon me in the day of trouble; I will deliver you, and you will honor me."

God desires us to be totally honest with Him so He can minister to all our needs. We should pour out the inner needs and anxieties of our hearts, as well as our eternal needs. Only then, as we are touched with His power, will we become whole and full of His life.

e. Intercession for Others

1 Timothy 2:1-4: "I urge, then, first of all, that requests, prayers, intercession and thanksgiving be made for everyone—for kings and all those in authority, that we may live peaceful and quiet lives in all godliness and holiness. This is good, and pleases God our Saviour, who wants all men to be saved and to come to a knowledge of the truth."

D. Praying for Leaders
(Adapted from the article "Praying for Leaders" by C. Peter Wagner)
This article says:

The most under-utilized source of spiritual power in our church is intercession for Christian leaders.

1. What is Intercession?

Exodus 17:8-13 records Joshua's victory in the battle against Amalek. As Joshua went into battle, Moses climbed up on the hill to intercede for him. Whenever Moses' arms were up, Joshua was winning, but when Moses' arms went down, Joshua was losing. Aaron and Hur helped Moses keep his arms up and ultimately, Joshua was victorious.

While Joshua's name is recorded in military history, the real battle was taking place in the heavenlies, where Moses was fighting. Both types of warfare were needed for victory. Joshua was the leader doing the ministry while Moses was the intercessor engaged in spiritual warfare.

2. Three Types of Intercessors

a. Intercessors who have remote contact with the leader.
There are highly visible leaders who have hundreds of people who have been called by God to pray for him or her everyday, but who have never met him or her personally. This prayer power is very important, especially for those who enjoy a "celebrity" status.

b. Intercessors who maintain a casual contact with the leader.
They are typically those who say when they shake the pastor's hand, "Pastor, I pray for you everyday."

c. Intercessors who enjoy close contact with the leader.
The number is usually limited to one or two. They usually keep very close contact with the leader and they have knowledge of very personal issues in the leader's life.

SPONSOR'S SHARE TIMES

Each week during the training, you are expected to meet with another Cell Leader Intern and hold each other accountable for the reading assignments and ministry activities you perform inside your cell groups.

This is not meant to impose a burden, but rather a blessing upon you! It is suggested that you arrange to meet either just before or just after the weekly training session. Sometimes this has involved nothing more than just "finding a corner" where you can share for a half hour or so, or it might involve having a snack together.

Each week, there are three books you will be reading: this one, the *Shepherd's Guidebook*, and *Ordering Your Private World*. If you are not a "fast reader," here are some tips for you:

1. Scan the assigned chapters, underlining thoughts you want to remember.
2. Look particularly for the answers to questions provided in this section.
3. Think of special areas which have impacted you as you have read the materials which you would like to discuss with your sponsor.

When you meet, each of you might begin your time by sharing one key thought you have grasped or one area you are struggling with. Together, decide on what you want to focus on in the brief time you have. You may wish to contact your Trainer before or after the session to discuss any areas where you feel you need help.

The remainder of these pages are prepared to stimulate your thinking as you read through the materials. Heartfelt thanks for the condensations of the two books which appeared in Hatfield's *Cell Leader's Guidebook* which have been used to prepare the materials which follow.

SHEPHERD'S GUIDEBOOK
CHAPTERS 1-2

1. A true cell group is suspended between two poles. Select them from the list below:
   - ☐ A compelling desire to bear witness to the cell's life in Christ.
   - ☐ A search for friendships that does not obligate me too much.
   - ☐ The quality of Spirit-guided relationships.

2. Give a title to each person in this diagram (see page 16):

3. A cell should begin with ____ to ____ people and should never have more than ____ people in it.

4. As a cell leader, your primary task is to:
   - ☐ Facilitate
   - ☐ Teach

5. How does Numbers 27:15-17 refer to your ministry?

   Moses said to the LORD, "May the LORD, the God of the spirits of all mankind, appoint a man over this community to go out and come in before them, one who will lead them out and bring them in, so the LORD's people will not be like sheep without a shepherd."

   _____

6. Rate your potential to grow into these areas of servanthood:
   (0 = Weak; 5 = Needs work; 10 = Ready to do this now)

Guiding	____
Nurturing	____
Protecting	____
Caring for needs	____
Equipping all cell members	____

126

7. What is a "Type A" unbeliever? _____

8. What is a "Type B" unbeliever? _____

9. What would you like to discuss when you meet with your fellow Cell Leader Intern in your get-together?

ORDERING YOUR PRIVATE WORLD
PREFACE THROUGH CHAPTER 2

Which ones of these statements are true for you?

- ☐ "I'm so disorganized!
- ☐ "I can't get my act together!"
- ☐ "My inner life is a mess!"
- ☐ "My private life is a failure!"

1. What does the term "private world" refer to?

- ☐ Where self-esteem is forged.
- ☐ Where basic decisions about values are made.
- ☐ Where we commune with God
- ☐ All of the above

2. The private world can be divided into five sections. Which ones are your greatest challenge?

- ☐ 1. I am driven, not a person called into ministry.
- ☐ 2. I do not organize my limited time to fulfill my priorities.
- ☐ 3. I do not discipline my mind.
- ☐ 4. My spirit, the "garden" of my private world, needs attention.
- ☐ 5. I need to rest, to keep a "sabbath peace.

3. What is the "Sinkhole Syndrome?"

_____
_____
_____

4. MacDonald says it is dangerous for Christians to work hard, shoulder massive responsibilities, yet ignore the private side of their lives. Underneath the activity there is nothing that is solid and dependable. Sooner or later these believers burn out.

As you have read these first chapters, have you seen a "danger zone" in your own life? Is the source of your ministry as a cell leader the indwelling Christ, flowing like a river of living water? Or, are you seeking to do His work without His presence?

SHEPHERD'S GUIDEBOOK
CHAPTERS 3-4

1. List the five stages that a cell group will pass through:
   STAGE 1: _____
   STAGE 2: _____
   STAGE 3: _____
   STAGE 4: _____
   STAGE 5: _____

2. What is a "triad?" _____

3. What is "role playing?"_____

4. How will you use "feedback" as a cell leader?
   _____

5. How will you apply the instructions about physical surroundings in arranging the rooms where your cell group meets?
   ☐ Arrive early and reset the room to be appropriate for the group.
   ☐ Instruct the entire cell group about the importance of physical surroundings.
   ☐ Both of the above.

6. Meditate on ways you will implement these keys for building a successful fellowship in your cell group; share your thoughts with your co-worker when you next meet:
   • Submission to God's word.
   • Unconditional acceptance for each member.
   • Absolute forgiveness for each member.
   • Genuine support and total confidentiality.
   • Edification as a primary goal.

7. Can you write from memory the four parts of facilitating?
   1. _____
   2. _____
   3. _____
   4. _____

8. What are the three basic response patterns given for us to apply in 1Thessalonians 5:14?
   1. Admonish the _____
   2. Encourage the _____
   3. Help the _____

9. With which of the above would you . . .
   CHALLENGE? ____
   CHEER? ____
   CARRY? ____

ORDERING YOUR PRIVATE WORLD
CHAPTERS 3-5

1. Below are listed the symptoms of a "driven" person. On a scale of 1 to 10, (1 = low, 10 - high), rate yourself:

   1. Most often gratified only by accomplishment: _____
   2. Preoccupied with the symbols of accomplishment: _____
   3. Usually caught in the uncontrollable pursuit of expansion: _____
   4. Have a limited regard for integrity, push ahead: _____
   5. Possess limited or undeveloped people skills: _____
   6. Highly competitive: _____
   7. Possesses a volcanic force of anger: _____
   8. Usually abnormally busy: _____

2. How many of these reasons for being "driven" apply to you?

   ☐ Growing up in an environment where "well done" was never heard.

   ☐ An early experience of serious deprivation or shame.

   ☐ Being raised in an environment where being driven is a way of life.

3. How do you respond to these words from the book?

   "To people like this, an ordered private world has little meaning. The only thing worth giving attention to is the public world, where things can be measured, admired and used."

   "To deal with being driven, one must begin to ruthlessly appraise one's motives and values. One can be called upon to lay down some of the activities in this life—things that are not necessarily bad, but that have been important for all the wrong reasons."

   _____

   _____

4. The text goes on to describe the "called" person. How many of these statements apply to you?

   ☐ The called person has a clear sense of purpose.

   ☐ The called person understands commitment

5. Becoming "called" requires a "desert experience," a place and a time when we withdraw from the habits and pressures that have ordered our lives in the past. Have you ever had a "desert experience?" Is it time for you to withdraw and have a quiet time in an extended "Listening Room?" Can you imagine what it would mean to yourself, your family, and your cell group if your sense of "call" became greater and greater?

SHEPHERD'S GUIDEBOOK
CHAPTERS 5-6

1. Developing others calls us to *model*, to *mentor*, those in our cell group. Does your present lifestyle include these nine steps? (*Check those that are true for you at this time*):

☐ I allow others to first watch me.

☐ I then explain what I did, and why I did it.

☐ I observe as my apprentice does what I did.

☐ I objectively explain strengths and weaknesses observed.

☐ I provide remedial activity to strengthen the weaknesses.

☐ I turn the task over to my apprentice.

☐ I use "benign neglect," enabling my apprentice to take hold.

☐ I closely monitor as my apprentice develops an apprentice.

☐ I remain a close friend, treating my apprentice as my equal.

2. Do you use these indicators of spiritual growth?

☐ My apprentice is not as much controlled by circumstances as in charge of them.

☐ My apprentice is responsible and dependable.

☐ My apprentice reflects a God-centered value system.

☐ My apprentice puts the cell group ahead of work, school, and family time.

ORDERING YOUR PRIVATE WORLD
CHAPTERS 6-7

1. How many of these symptoms of disorganization exist in your life?

    ☐ My desk, kitchen counter, workroom, etc. is cluttered.

    ☐ My car is in poor condition.

    ☐ I am aware of a lessening of my self-esteem.

    ☐ I forget appointments, telephone calls, and miss deadlines.

    ☐ I tend to spend my energies on unproductive tasks.

    ☐ I have a tendency to daydream, avoid decisions, procrastinate.

    ☐ My will to work steadily decreases; excellency is affected.

    ☐ I feel poor about my world.

    ☐ I really do not enjoy intimacy, never have time to be with God.

2. These laws of unseized time apply to me:

    ☐ I don't have a clear sense of mission; I do things I am not good at instead of investing my time where my strengths lie.

    ☐ I am governed by the urgent, constantly putting out "fires."

    ☐ I am strongly influenced by dominant people in my life.

    ☐ I tend to invest unseized time in things that gain public acclaim.

3. I use these ways to recapture my time and bring order to my life:

    ☐ I use my rhythms of maximum effectiveness.
    ☐ I have good criteria for choosing how to use my time.
    ☐ I command time by budgeting it in advance.

SHEPHERD'S GUIDEBOOK
CHAPTERS 7-8

1. Draw lines to connect the people described in the left column to the appropriate *Year of Equipping Courses* listed in the right column. *(See page 71 to check your answers.)*

LITTLE CHILDREN	New Believers Station
New Believer	Welcome To Your New Life
Ready for Service	The Shepherd's Guidebook
PROBLEMED PERSONS	Touching Hearts Guidebook
Cold Christian	Building Bridges, Opening Hearts
Lukewarm Christian	Cover the Bible
Emotionally Damaged	The Arrival Kit
EQUIPPING FOR SERVICE	Sponsor's Guidebook
For Everyone	Search for Significance
Young Men	Building Awareness, Opening Hearts
Fathers	Cell Leader's Guidebook
Wider Ministry (Cell Leader)	Building Groups, Opening Hearts

2. Prepare to discuss the diagrams on page 75 with your Partner. What example of each diagram can you share?

3. Prepare your own Intercessory Prayer List if you have not already done so *(see page 81)* and share it with your Partner.

4. What did Roger Mitchell mean when he said, "Spiritual warfare is the hidden face of evangelism . . ."?

5. Before the cell leader prays it is important to know the will of God concerning a situation. Prayer becomes a "Listening Room" experience. It is not possible to proceed effectively without having a deep awareness that further praying is being done according to God's plan. Then, with absolute assurance, the "binding on earth what is bound in heaven" takes place.

In the space below, jot down one experience of this truth you would like to share with your Partner when you next meet:

_____

_____

6. Prayer chains are a vital tool to a group. Please rate the effectiveness of the prayer chain in your present cell group:

☐ Very effective   ☐ Moderately so   ☐ Needs attention

7. List the names of people in your present cell who need prayer for:

A deeper hunger for God: _____

A lifestyle impervious to Christ: _____

A greater level of faith _____

A key individual God will use _____

A new sensitivity to unsaved _____

8. Peter Lord writes in *The 2959 Plan*,

It is honoring to God when our immediate and first response to any situation is to consult Him. It is very dishonoring to God when we make Him our last choice. Have you ever heard someone say, "We have done all we can; we might as well pray."? If we are going to "acknowledge Him in all our ways" and "seek first the Kingdom of God," one of the best ways is to make Him our consultant and advisor."

What is your desire today related to your prayer life?

_____

ORDERING YOUR PRIVATE WORLD
CHAPTERS 8-9

TRUE FALSE

☐ ☐ To be in front at the first turn in a race is meaningless without the endurance to finish strongly.

☐ ☐ The ordering of our private world does not require strong mental endurance and intellectual growth.

☐ ☐ Being out of shape mentally causes us to become dependent on the thoughts and opinions of others.

☐ ☐ There is not connection between intelligence and minds that are not strengthened.

☐ ☐ It is not necessary to train our minds. It is possible to coast on natural talent and not develop our minds.

☐ ☐ As Christians we have been given the mind of Christ.

☐ ☐ We do not grow by listening to mentors or critics.

☐ ☐ Paul revealed his respect for growing through reading by asking Timothy for parchments and books.

☐ ☐ Defensive study is exploring, turning up truth from many sources.

☐ ☐ Offensive study is restricted to one chosen subject.

☐ ☐ When we take seriously the growth and development of our minds we come to know God more fully, and are infinitely more useful in the service of others.

What thoughts would you like to share when you meet with your Partner this week?

_____

_____

SHEPHERD'S GUIDEBOOK
CHAPTERS 9-10

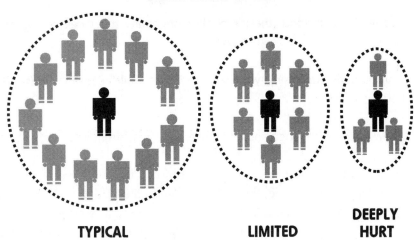

| TYPICAL | LIMITED | DEEPLY HURT |

1. Name one person you know who fits each of these *oikoses:*

   TYPICAL: _____

   LIMITED: _____

   DEEPLY HURT: _____

2. Evaluate your present cell group after reading this paragraph:

   "Kinning" is creating true Christian community. It is home, where you are always welcome no matter what stupid decision you have made in the past or present. It's a place where crotchety, disagreeable, thankless old sinners are welcomed and challenged to be free from their inner strongholds. Praise and worship shapes the group's personality. The Lord's Supper, prayer and edification are vital to its lifestyle. It is also constantly reaching out to others until multiplication occurs.

   Would you say your cell group has reached this level of life and ministry?

   ☐ Yes   ☐ Not yet

   What can you do to move it forward into a deeper level?

3. An effective cell leader shows *consistency*. Here are some of the traits of a consistent leader. Tick the ones that apply to you:

☐ Loving all, not some, of the group.

☐ Caring as much about the life of the community this week as you did last week.

☐ Transparently confessing your own shortfalls while revealing your growing faith.

☐ Knowing when to let go and let people grow apart from you.

4. If you look at the evidence, it becomes obvious that whenever, wherever a person has a hunger for God, they are easily led to the Lord, but for others seeds must be planted and watered before there is a harvest. The assignment of your cell group is to focus on the planting and watering, knowing that the harvest is simply plucking ripe fruit. *How can you share this concept with your cell group when the cell leader turns over the next Share The Vision time to you?*

_____

_____

5. Roger Mitchell in *The Kingdom Factor* writes, "It was not only the words that Jesus said that revealed the Father's glory, but the works that He did." List below two instances you have observed where God has worked in your cell group in a way that witnesses to His power (e.g., a healing of a body, a release from a stronghold, etc.) . . .

_____

_____

6. What is the difference between a *share group* and an *interest group*? (see pages 101-following):

_____

_____

ORDERING YOUR PRIVATE WORLD
CHAPTERS 10-11

1. Chapter 10 points out that the center of our private world is our *spirit*. While it is eternal, it can exist in a state of such disorganization that almost no communion with God is possible. Here are signs of a disorganized spirit. Check any which you feel are true of you:

   ☐ I do not feel I have a true friendship with the Christ in me.

   ☐ I really do not feel I am accountable to God for my life.

   ☐ Being His son or daughter is not significant to my value system.

   ☐ I have little reserve or resolve in crisis moments.

2. These are four spiritual exercises that are of fundamental importance. How many of them are true of you?

   ☐ I have periods of solitude and silence.

   ☐ I listen to God daily and journal my thoughts.

   ☐ Reflection and meditation are important to me.

   ☐ I enjoy prayer as worship and intercession.

3. Some equate silence and solitude with laziness, inaction, and unproductivity. Have you deliberately found the time and place that fits your personal temperament? If so, write it below and share it with your Partner:

   _____

4. What would you like to share with your Partner from your journaling? Some things may be very private, but are there areas of your journal you could share? Would you be blessed by learning more of your partner's journal as well? Select a passage from your journal to share when next you meet together.

SHEPHERD'S GUIDEBOOK
CHAPTERS 11-12

1. Strongholds in the lives of believers are often gone unchallenged. They must be discerned by the cell leader and ministry provided. Here are the steps you will face in short term crisis situations. If you have already experienced one or more of them, tick the boxes to indicate them:

   ☐ A person in shock and disbelief says, "Why did God . . .?"

   ☐ A person is overcome by the circumstances and cannot think rationally. Decision making is related to survival.

   ☐ Days or weeks later, the cell leader can talk about the situation and help new truths to be grasped. The cell meetings are invaluable at this stage.

2. Look over the stress events listed on page 117 of the *Shepherd's Guidebook*. Underline the stresses that now exist in your own life. Discuss them with your Partner.

3. What is "transference?" (See page 119). Have you ever felt an inappropriate attraction to someone? How did you handle it? This is an area for you and your Partner to discuss, and perhaps agree to hold one another accountable for support. It is a disastrous thing when those serving the Lord allow their feelings to run unbridled and for sin to occur!

4. Concerning the ministry to children in your cell group: which of these conditions are effectively taking place at present?

   ☐ Parents model Kingdom relationships to the children in the cell.

   ☐ The children feel they truly belong to the life of the cell.

   ☐ There is great sensitivity among the adults to the needs of the children, and a sincere desire for the children to be encouraged in their walk with Christ.

ORDERING YOUR PRIVATE WORLD
CHAPTERS 12-13

1. The things we hear in the Listening Room must be internalized. This is done through *reflection* and *meditation*. Not until we automatically respond without thinking about it is a value embedded in our nature.

   Reflection places us in the middle of a circumstance or story, and requires us to see ourselves as involved. *Meditation* is when we allow words to trickle down over the structures of our inner being as we repeat them over and over. This is the reason scripture memory is so critical.

   Two reasons who people struggle when it comes to prayer are listed below. Tick the boxes of those which are true for you:

   ☐ Worship and intercession seem to be unnatural acts. Prayer seems to be a form of inaction, and we desire to be active.

   ☐ Worship and intercession seem to be admissions of weakness. Prayer in its most authentic form acknowledges that we are weak and dependent upon our God.

2. This is the pattern MacDonald suggests for the contents of prayer: *Adoration, Confession, Intercession*. Jot down one thought related to each of these areas that would help you discuss the way your prayer life operates when you next share with your Partner:

   ADORATION: _____

   _____

   CONFESSION:_____

   _____

   INTERCESSION: _____

   _____

SHEPHERD'S GUIDEBOOK
CHAPTERS 13-14

1. Your own pattern of stewardship is going to become glaringly obvious to your cell group members. In Chapter 13, there are examples of how the early Christians used God's money. Evaluate your own patterns of using His funds by jotting down answers to the questions below. Share them with your Partner.

   • How have I ministered to others through financial aid?

   _____

   • How have I supported the pastoral team in our cell church?

   _____

   • How have I helped support new work or sister churches?

   _____

2. Do you have a "second source" of wealth? (See page 141). Do you believe it is possible to live by this trilogy?

   It is the task of a servant to obey his Master.
   It is the obligation of the Master to provide for that servant.
   Therefore, the servant will never lack what is needed.

3. Can you list below the four stages that a cell group will go through?
   (If you need help, see pages 148-149)

   Stage 1: _____

   Stage 2: _____

   Stage 3: _____

   Stage 4: _____

4. Prepare to review the ten week cell group cycle on page 151 in *The Shepherd's Guidebook* with your Partner. If any portion of it needs further explanation, ask your Trainer about it.

5. With your Partner, discuss *Triads, Role Playing,* and the use of *Feedback.*

6. Which of these non-verbal signals have you identified in cell group sessions?

☐ Boredom   ☐ Shame or embarrassment

☐ Defensiveness   ☐ Signs of anxiety

ORDERING YOUR PRIVATE WORLD
CHAPTER 14

1. There are three principles of genuine rest implied in the sabbath rest. As you meditate on them, tick the boxes of those that are true for you:

☐ I interpret my work and its meaning as dedicated to God.

☐ I daily sort out the truths and commitments of my life.

☐ I look forward to tomorrow and the ministry God is giving me.

2. To share with your Partner, jot down in the space below the most important single truth you gleaned from reading Chapter 14:

_____

_____

_____

_____

_____

SHEPHERD'S GUIDEBOOK
CHAPTERS 15-17

1. On page 161, meditate on the hidden agendas in cell groups. Can you think of one example of how a personal need in the life of one person impacted a cell meeting?

2. At this moment, what is an underlying cell group need that is a "hidden agenda" in your meetings?

3. Which ones of the four "W's" do you feel least prepared to lead in your cell group sessions? Share it with both your cell leader and your Partner. Seek to overcome this deficiency. Review pages 170-173 if necessary.

4. How would you explain to someone who knows nothing about the ministry of a cell leader the distinction between *teaching* and *facilitating?*

5. When you next meet with your Partner, discuss how you would deal with the the problem people described on pages 181-183:

JEFF: _____

MARY ANN:_____

GEORGE:_____

SARAH:_____

ROGER:_____

ALICE:_____

BILL AND BERTHA _____

DONNA:_____

142

INDEX

INDEX (Continued)